APPRECIATING INDIA'S MUSIC

An Introduction,
with an emphasis on the Music of South India.

by

EMMONS E. WHITE

CRESCENDO PUBLISHING COMPANY

BOSTON

Standard Book Number 87597-059-1
Library of Congress Card Number 70-131051
Printed in the United States of America
Copyright © 1971 by Crescendo Publishing Company

TABLE OF CONTENTS

Sri Tyagaraja, South Indian musician-composer
1767-1847

AUTHOR'S FOREWORD

This book was first published in the year 1957 by the Christian Literature Society of India for the use of Indian graduates who were preparing for service in the churches of India. Since returning to America I have felt it desirable to rewrite it, that it may be more helpful to Western readers.

My qualifications for writing it are: (1) a love for the classical music of southern India and (2) many years of study under professional Indian musicians in order to learn to sing its songs. That study began in the year 1922, about four years after my first arrival at Madurai, South India, as a missionary. In 1938 I specialized in the art of Kalakshepam, conducted many performances of it, and wrote a book about it in Tamil which was published in 1955.

In rewriting "Appreciating India's Music" I have omitted the chapters dealing with the use of the music in the rites of the Indian Churches and substituted a new chapter with some selected Indian songs in Western staff notation. The lists of ragas in the Appendix have been put in staff instead of Indian notation.

Throughout the book both Indian and Western musical terms have been used. The reader is warned that the corresponding terms used are not always identical in meaning. Such treatment is inevitable when one is trying to explain the culture of one country in terms of the culture of another. For example, in order to illustrate the beauties of Indian melodies, I have set down in Chapter IX a number of these melodies in staff notation. These notations are only rough skeletons of the originals, the exquisite beauty of which is largely dependent on the subtle embellishments that can be learned only from a competent teacher.

I have not dealt with the music of India as a whole. This book sets forth the types with which I am familiar. Those who seek a knowledge of the North Indian (Hindustani) music, or a knowledge of folk, dance and dramatic music should turn to other sources. (See Bibliography)

I am very grateful to the many people who, by their kind encouragement or technical assistance, have made possible both this book and my years of study of India's music. Space permits the acknowledgement of only a few of these friends.

i

First, I wish to express my thanks to the Christian Students' Library and the Christian Literature Society of India for permission to republish this book in its rewritten form.

Second, my especial thanks are due to Mr. D. Srinivasa Iyengar (Jalatarangam Vidwan) of Madurai, who has been my music teacher since 1940, and to Mr. D. Arthur Bhagavathar of Madurai, who trained me to perform my first Kalakshepam.

Third, special mention should be made of Miss Edith Thomas, Miss Edith Husted, and Mrs. Lois Allen of Claremont, California, who generously gave me technical help in notating the Indian songs in Chapter IX; to Mr. Amiya Das Gupta, Headmaster of the Sangeet School of Indian Music in Los Angeles for his kind help in the preparation of the list of Hindustani Ragas in the Appendix; to Mr. Howard Boatwright, Dean of the Music Department, Syracuse University, New York; to Mr. William F. Russell, Chairman of the Music Department, Pomona College, Claremont, California; and to Mr. Jon Higgins of the faculty, Wesleyan University, Middletown, Connecticut, for their expert advice and kind encouragement.

Last of all, I am grateful to my wife, whose knowledge of India and of Indian terminology and whose help in preparing and typing the entire manuscript have been of inestimable value to me.

In India as in every land there is popular music, most of which is here today and gone tomorrow. But music which springs from the soul of a people, such as the "Negro Spirituals" of America, or out of the brain and heart of a musical genius like the revered Tyagaraja of South India, can never die but will continue to reveal its beauties from generation to generation. As the poet Keats has written:

"A thing of beauty is a joy forever,
Its loveliness increases; it will never
Pass into nothingness . . . ."

Claremont, California   Emmons E. White
September 1970

CHAPTER I.

THE APPROACH

Whatever may be said about the status of music in other countries, there can be absolutely no doubt that it is woven into the very fabric of India's life. From the towering, snowcapped Himalayas at the extreme north to Cape Comorin two thousand miles south, and from Bengal on the east to Bombay on the west music may be heard at every hour of the day and night in that great subcontinent. One can hear the plaintive, carefree singing of the little shepherd boy as he pastures his cattle or goats in the fields or by the roadside, the song of the women as they plant rice in the fields, the chanteys of laborers as they tug together to hoist some piece of heavy timber into place, the shrill sounds of pipes and the loud thumping of drums at a wedding or some other social function, and the loud sustained singing of the oxcart driver as he goads his oxen along the public highway at night and lifts his voice on high to the starry sky. At different hours of the day or night the visitor may hear over the public-address system the music of some musician or opera magnified many times. Such occurrences — and they are many — will force him to form some kind of judgment about Indian music, whether favorable or unfavorable. There are many kinds of music — good and bad, classical and popular. It is not necessary to enjoy all kinds equally well. But the best music of any country is a cultural heritage which should be rightly valued by musicians everywhere. Such appreciation would no doubt contribute to international friendship and understanding, and so to the peace for which the world increasingly longs. This book is written in the earnest hope that it will be of help to that end.

Many Indians do appreciate their musical heritage. But when we turn to history we find that in Western countries there has been a considerable ignorance of India's music. When, toward the end of the 16th century, Western armies, traders and missionaries began to penetrate India, they apparently paid little attention to her music. Their first impression was that it was very different from the music of their homelands, and presumably inferior. Since such judgment was based upon ignorance,

1

it was superficial. As time went on, the world became more and more interested in India's art, architecture, paintings, handwork and religions. What world traveller has not heard of the palaces of the Moghul emperors, the famous paintings of Ajunta, the Buddhist stupas and the great Hindu temples of South India! Western scholars by their researches have created a permanent interest in such ancient Sanskrit writings as the Vedas and Upanishads, and such epic poems as the Mahabharata and the Ramayana. But India's music continued to be relatively unknown in the West until recently.

However, one must rejoice that of late things have improved. There is an encouraging increase in the number of people who are becoming interested in the subject. Their efforts have been assisted by a growing amount of scholarly research along the lines of archaeology, anthropology, sociology, comparative religion, ethnomusicology and other studies. During this century Western scholars like A. H. Fox-Strangways, Alain Danielou, Curt Sachs, and Herbert Popley have all made valuable contributions to the knowledge of India's music. The United Nations Educational, Social and Cultural Organization (UNESCO) provides an exchange of ideas and cultural heritage among the nations of the world. An international council of music has been founded at Paris. The United States Information Service (USIS) has been making a similar contribution. Even more encouraging is the fact that within the last decade, especially among the younger generation in the West, there has been a real growth of interest in India's music. Outstanding Indian musicians, like Ravi Shankar, have been attracting great audiences in America and elsewhere by their splendid public performances. Schools for training people in the various types of India's classical music have been recently set up in cities like Los Angeles and New York, and at Wesleyan University in Middletown, Connecticut.

Is it possible, for one to whom Indian music seems incomprehensible, to learn to appreciate it? This book answers the question. Its aim is to present the subject in a form which is clear, accurate, and attractive to a person who has neither the time nor the opportunity to study the subject under professional teachers. A simple answer to the question above would be that the student seek the opportunity to hear this music as often as possible and to listen without pre-judging it.

Many years ago a young American man was travelling with a friend by oxcart to a small village in India, where they were to meet a group of poor, under-privileged rural people. As they neared the village they were met by a messenger and were requested to proceed on foot to receive a special welcome in true Indian fashion. They were met by four drummers, who were clad only in loincloths and turbans. Each of the four men carried in his hands a tambourine-like drum and two slender drumsticks. The drummers then walked backward while escorting the visitors and drumming as they went. Never in his whole life had the young American heard such marvelous drumming. It was done with absolute

2

unity and precision, and with frequent changes in fascinating rhythmic patterns. It was like a brass band, grand opera and drum corps rolled into one. He began to realize then as never before that drumming could be a real art. Probably many an Indian village could boast of such local talent. It was a few years later that he heard similar drumming by the temple musicians of Kandy, Ceylon. Superb drumming, of course, is not the only value in Indian music, but it does play a significant part.

Melody also is an important component of India's music, as well as rhythm. These and other elements of the music will be discussed in some detail in the following chapters.

It is important that the Western student should, as far as possible, divest himself of all preconceptions about this music and sit down before it as open-minded as a little child. This will not be easy. The process will undoubtedly require much repetition and explanation. But let him possess his soul in patience! I resided in India more than two years before I fell in love with India's classical music and now cannot recall the exact date when it happened. This music is not to be studied in a mechanical, half-hearted way: like a mystical state it has to be experienced.

Another obvious but important fact needs to be stated at this point. People differ considerably in their capacity for appreciating good music. It has often been imagined that the ability to sing, or to play a musical instrument is ipso facto an indication of the presence of a capacity to appreciate the good music of any nation. This is not necessarily true. A performer of music may actually be more interested in displaying his technical skill or the quality of his voice than he is in the music he is performing.

In this age of radio, Hi-Fi, and television there are many who enjoy or use music as a background to something they are doing or experiencing. One hears soft soothing music in shops and supermarkets while one considers what to buy. Background music is often used in moving pictures to evoke in the spectator the emotions appropriate to the scenes which he is viewing. Many people can apparently carry on a conversation, or study a lesson, while keeping one ear open, as it were, to music which is being performed near them.

But the best music of any country cannot be appreciated in any such superficial way. It should command the hearer's *full attention*. It is best appreciated when it involves the whole being of the listener. One must also realize there are indeed many people who, though they may not be able to sing or to play a musical instrument well, have within themselves a real capacity to enjoy good music. It is among this type of listener, and not merely among singers or players that India's music will find its true audience.

Another difficulty which may face the Western musician who wishes to understand Indian music is its lack of staff notation. Up to the present time there has been no agreed system of notation in India by which classical music can be transcribed. The student must realize that this music has been transmitted orally by teacher to pupil for many generations. In modern times Indian musicians have attempted to record these melodies in the Indian *sol-fa* (Sa-Ri-Ga) notation using certain Indian symbols. The *Sa-Ri-Ga* system is given in some detail in the Appendix of this book. Still more recently many performances by Indian musicians have been recorded on Hi-Fi or stereo, or on recording tape. This is a much more satisfactory medium, since it reproduces the embellishments of the melodies without which the music cannot be fully understood. Such recordings are now available both in India and the West.

A few musicians (mostly Western) have tried their hand at recording this music in staff notation but without much success. The author has made such an attempt in Chapter IX, but warns the reader not to be content with such renderings. The technical difficulties involved will become apparent as one goes deeply into the subject. The reader who tries to play or to sing the melodies in Chapter IX is cautioned not to set them to Western harmonies in the usual way, but to use the *drone-chord* indicated as the only accompaniment. The musician who does use the Western harmonies is not really playing Indian music.

What are the prerequisites for learning to appreciate this music? They may be summarized thus: (1) *an open mind,* (2) *the ability to carry a tune,* (3) *a good sense of rhythm,* and (4) *a willingness to spend some time, effort and money in acquiring a good knowledge of it.*

People sometimes ask which kind of music is superior, Indian or Western. How answer such a question dogmatically? It would be like asking which kind of food is superior, meat-and-potatoes, or rice-and-curry. The answer should be, each kind has its own delicious flavor. There are people who enjoy both kinds, without bothering to ask such a question. To ask such a question might be like asking which is the superior athlete, a mile runner or a baseball pitcher. Both are important types of athletes. In the same way it is quite possible for a person born in a given type of racial culture to come to appreciate that of another, while retaining an appreciation of his own. Thus he can learn to enjoy the beautiful melodies of the famous South Indian musician Tyagaraja, while retaining at the same time his love for the music of Bach or Beethoven. There exist today both Indian and Westerners who are examples of this statement. Only as one learns to value the musical standards of a culture other than his own, and to measure that culture by its own standards, as Captain Day has well said, will he be able to judge what is good and admirable in that culture.

In conclusion, four ways of mastering this subject are presented to the beginner.

First, he should learn to sing or play an Indian instrument under the tutelage of an expert Indian musician. With the help of such a teacher he could learn to perform a bit of the music of the great masters. As he practises, over and over again, the tonal beauties of such music will begin to unfold. This is undoubtedly the best way of appreciation. But it might not be practicable for a Western student, since the necessary teachers are not easily available in the West.

Second, wherever possible he should attend public concerts of such music. This is now increasingly possible in the big cities of the West. He should remain at such concerts throughout the entire performance if possible, in order to absorb their excellences. It would be very helpful if some one who was knowledgeable in the art could sit with him to explain these. This would be a very valuable way of approach.

Third, commercial companies, both in India and in the West, are now producing excellent recordings of this music by top artists. The student should buy some of these recordings and play and listen to them frequently.

Last of all, for those who would delve more deeply into the technical and theoretical aspects of the subject, there are a number of scholarly works written by both Indian and Western musicologists. To supply this need a bibliography has been included in the Appendix of this book. Unfortunately many of these books fairly bristle with Indian terminology which may serve rather to bewilder the unfamiliar student. To help meet this situation a Glossary has also been included in the Appendix, giving the meaning of a number of such terms.

A word of caution must be given. Not all the mastery of technical terms, or of the physics and mathematics of the subject — no matter how ably or correctly presented — can take the place of that knowledge which comes *through direct listening to the music and through an ability to perform some of it.*

CHAPTER II
ORIGIN AND HISTORY

Music is older than recorded history. Its origin is lost in the mists of antiquity and legend. It is probable that the first music consisted of song, but the earliest stages of its evolution are still unknown. India is rich in folk, dance, dramatic and classical music.

In India from the earliest times music has been closely associated with religion. In particular it was associated with the *Sama Veda,* one of the four ancient books of the Hindu religion which are written in Sanskrit. Scholars hold that parts of the Vedas were already in writing when the Aryan tribes began to invade India from the northwest between 2000 and 1000 B.C. While the high priest conducted the solemn rite of the Soma drink-offering to God, using the *Atharva Veda,* another priest is said to have sung chants from the *Sama Veda.* In Hindu temples today one can still hear chants in praise of the deity which doubtless originated in very ancient times.

Hindus believe that the art of music is especially patronized by the goddess Saraswati, the consort of Brahma. She is often pictured or represented in the form of an image seated upon a lotus flower and playing upon a stringed instrument. Rev. H. A. Popley has written:

In Hindu mythology the various departments of life and learning are usually associated with different *rishis,* and so to one of them is traced the first instructions that men have received in the art of music. *Bharata Rishi* is said to have taught the art to the heavenly dancers (Apsarasas) who afterward performed before the god Siva. The rishi Narada, who wandered about the earth and heaven singing and playing his *Vina,* taught music to men. *

Bharata Rishi lived sometime between the fifth century B.C. and 100 A.D. He composed a scientific treatise called Natya Sastra, which set forth the principles of Indian music that then prevailed and dealt with the art of dancing. This scientific work is said to have survived the ravages of time.

* Popley, MUSIC OF INDIA, p.7

7

Indian musicians have sometimes claimed that a deity resides in each of the seven main tones of the scale. There is an interesting story from the *Ramayana,* one of the two great epic poems composed in the early centuries of the Christian era. The story is told that Hanuman, king of the monkeys, boasted to Prince Rama, the hero of the Ramayana, about his skill in song. Rama determined that he should be humbled. There was a certain rishi living in a jungle who by his occult powers had caused seven lovely nymphs to live each in one of the seven main notes of the scale. One day Rama took Hanuman to a spot near the rishi's abode and induced him to play on the Vina and to sing. While this went on, the seven nymphs happened to pass on their way to bring water from a spring. When Hanuman sang one of the notes incorrectly, the nymph connected with that particular note dropped dead. As soon as the rishi heard the bad singing, he came out of his house smiling, took up the Vina, and played all seven notes correctly. As he did so, the dead nymph came to life again, and gaily joined her companions. So runs the legend.

Another famous figure of antiquity was the musician Panini. He lived in northern India in the third century B.C. during the time of Alexander the Great of Macedonia. It is interesting to note the relationship between the Indian and the Greek musical systems.

Turning from ancient times to modern days, historical evidence demonstrates that Indian music was closely connected with temple rituals, and that it was patronized by rajahs and men of wealth. In the early Christian era the Chola kings of the country north of Tanjore, the Pandiya kings of Madurai, South India, and the Chera kings in that part of India now known as the State of Kerala, were patrons of the arts and of music.

The *Silappadigaram* (300 A.D.), a classic Tamil dramatic poem, mentions the drummer, the flute player and the Vina, as well as the lute and also specimens of Tamil songs. It also contains some of the earliest expositions of the Indian musical scale, giving the notes of the gamut, and also a number of the modes and *ragas* in use at that time. The names given to the notes are not those current at the present day and are with one exception pure Tamil words. *

From the fourth to the sixth centuries A.D. the famous Hindu Gupta kings reigned in North India. Their reign was called "The Golden Age", during which the arts and music were patronized by them. The great poet-musician Kalidasa lived at that time. The western *sol-fa* system dates from the time of Guido De Arezzo (tenth century). But there are evidences in South India that the Indian musical scales are still older. An interesting stone inscription, dating back to the seventh cen-

---

* Popley, MUSIC OF INDIA, p. 1.

8

tury has been discovered in Pudukottai, South India, which proves that, under the reigning Pallava kings, certain definite musical scales were then in use.

The great Tamil classic poem, *Tiru Kural,* composed about 500 A.D., mentions certain musical instruments in the following verse:

"Sweet sound the flute and the lute
To those who know not the melody
Of their little ones' prattle." *

Captain C. R. Day writes that the most flourishing stage of Indian music was during the period of the Hindu rajahs and until the eighth century. At that time the foreign Muslim armies were beginning to invade India from the northwest. In general the invaders were interested only in their native Persian and Arabic music and not in the traditional type of Hindu music. From 1000 to about 1400 A.D. a fusion began to take place of the Persian and Arabian music with Hindu music. At the close of that period the Northern (Hindustani) School of music (which included the new mixed music) and the Southern (Carnatic) School of music began to emerge. Each school developed its own separate rules and nomenclatures. Present-day scholars are not agreed on the question of whether this separate development has been in the best interests of India's music.

The new Muslim rulers of India were not able to unite all of India in one empire, as Emperor Asoka had done in the third century B.C. They became established in North India about the year 1200 A.D. Hindu rajahs in other parts of India continued to hold out against them. One such region was the Deccan in Central India, where from 1330 to 1634 the famous Vijayanagar kings reigned, under whose patronage music was encouraged. When Firoz Shah became Sultan in the North in 1236, however, he invited musicians and dancing girls from all over India to perform at his court in Delhi. North Indian music continued to develop differently from South Indian music during this period.

Two celebrated musicians of that time were *Sarngadeva* and *Jeyadeva.* The former lived at the court of the Yadawa Dynasty in the Deccan. At that time the famous Maratha (Hindu) empire extended as far south as the Kaveri River. Sarngadeva probably came into contact with both the Northern and the Southern types of music. He wrote a very technical work in Sanskrit called the *Sangita Ratnakara,* which shows signs of this contact. The book is said to deal with the whole range of musical forms and compositions, but scholars disagree significantly about the system described in the Sangita Ratnakara.

Jeyadeva was a great devotee of the god Krishna. He was a Brahman by caste, resided at the court of King Lakshmanasina of Bengal, and was one of the earliest of Bengal poets. His chief work is the Sanskrit

* Book VII, Verse 4, Translated by E. E. White

9

poem entitled "Gita Govinda". It contains about twenty-four songs on the theme of the love of Krishna for the maid Radha. The poem stresses the union of the individual soul with the Universal Soul. Each of the songs is based upon a particular raga and tala. (See Chapters IV and V for the meaning of these terms.)

The greatest development of music in North India took place under the patronage of the celebrated Moghul (Muslim) emperors, who ruled at Delhi from the 14th to the 17th centuries. At the beginning of that period there was a famous singer at the court of Sultan Ali-ud-din (1295-1316) named Amir Khusru. This musician introduced the mode of singing which is a mixture of Persian and Indian models, as well as several of the modern *ragas*. He is said to have introduced and adapted from Persia the *Sitar*, a stringed instrument common in North Indian music. The great Emperor Akbar, who reigned from 1542 to 1605, was an exceedingly broadminded and tolerant monarch. He was deeply interested in science, religion and the arts. He supported at his court a renowned musician named Tan Sen, whose master at Brindaban, Haridas Swami, was an even greater musician. The following is one of the many interesting stories told about Tan Sen.

After one of Tan Sen's performances the emperor asked him if there were any musician in the world who was greater than he. Tan Sen replied that there was indeed one who far surpassed him. At once the emperor was eager to hear this other singer. When he was told that this other musician would refuse to obey the emperor's command to come, the emperor asked to be taken to him. He went disguised as a servant of Tan Sen carrying his master's musical instrument. They came to the hermitage of Haridas Swami on the banks of the Jumna River. When Tan Sen asked his master to sing, he refused. Then Tan Sen played a little trick. He sang a song to his master, deliberately making a slight mistake. The master at once noted the mistake and showed his pupil how to sing the music correctly and then went on in a wonderful burst of melody. The emperor listened enraptured. Afterwards, when they were returning to the palace, the emperor said to Tan Sen, "Why cannot you sing like that?" "I have to sing whenever my emperor commands," replied Tan Sen, "but my master sings only in obedience to the inner voice." *

Another outstanding musician of that age was Purandara Das (1484-1564). In the musical history of India he is ranked with the great Tyagaraja. He was of Brahman parentage and is said to have been born as an answer to prayer. At the age of forty, through the influence of his pious wife, he became a convert to Vaishnavism. He is said to have composed the incredible number of 475,000 songs, in which the essence of Hindu scriptural teaching was presented. He was also a teacher of music. In his day music pupils began their study by learning to intone and sing in the ancient raga called *Maya-malava-goula*. (See Chapter IV)

* Popley — MUSIC OF INDIA, pp. 16-17.

Not long before this period the Maratha dynasty, as we have already noted, came to power in West India and fought against the Muslim rulers. With the spread of Muslim power over the greater part of India, Hindu music began to move westward and southward. One of the Maratha kings, who resided at Tanjore, South India, did so much for the cause of Indian music, that that city has since become one of the recognized musical centers for all India.

In the 17th century there lived at Tanjore a musical scholar named Pandit Vengatamakhi. It was he who formulated the 12-tone scale system and the 72 Primary Ragas of the Carnatic system. Many musical geniuses were born and flourished in South India during the years from 1750-1850. The three greatest lived in or near Tanjore. They were: Tyagaraja (1767-1847), Muthusamy Dikshitar (1776-1835), and Syama Sastri (1762-1827). Of these great men Mr. Sambamoorthy writes: "All three were devotees who spoke to God, and to whom God spoke". *

Of the three, Tyagaraja is the most famous. He made the greatest contribution to Carnatic music. Like so many other celebrated Indian musicians, he was born of Brahman parentage. Although Tanjore is in the Tamil-speaking area of Madras State, his mother tongue was Telegu, another Dravidian language. Because Telegu is so euphonious, it has been called the Italian of South Indian languages. Mr. Sambamoorthy writes that Tyagaraja was as significant for Carnatic music as Beethoven was for European music. He has composed very many beautiful songs. In fact, no South Indian singer of repute today will give a public performance without including several of Tyagaraja's classical songs in his repertoire. It was Tyagaraja who set the pattern for many a Carnatic raga. He also introduced and elaborated the characteristics of *sangati*. (See the glossary.) This is one reason why it is difficult for an untrained singer to sing many of his songs. Tyagaraja was a musical genius. He possessed the unique ability to compose not only music, but words which are particularly adapted to his melodies. This uniqueness is especially evident when one tries to adapt other words to his tunes, or to translate them into other languages. The result is not nearly so happy as the original!

In his early youth Tyagaraja was noted also for his religious zeal. He was a devout worshipper of Rama. In fact, most of his songs are in praise of Rama, or invoke Rama's blessing. There is a legend which holds that when Tyagaraja was eighteen years old, a Vaishnavite ascetic came from the city of Kanchipuram to see him and asked him to recite the name of Rama 960 million times. At that time Tyagaraja was married. He and his wife took this as a command of God and together set to work to fulfill it. At the rate of 125,000 times each day they recited the

---

* Sambamoorthy, GREAT COMPOSERS, Book I, p. 61.

name of Rama, until within 21 years they had finished this task. In these days of increasing secularism such thorough-going religious devotion will seem incredible to many.

Tyagaraja was held in great honor in his day. He lived the life of extreme austerity, having no wealth or property. Kings could neither command his services, nor induce him by gifts or remuneration to become a court musician. He absolutely refused to abandon his way of life. He sang or composed songs as the spirit moved him. Long before his death musicians came from all parts of India to meet him and listen to his singing. He warmly welcomed and encouraged musical talent among those who visited him, and graciously gave advice and help to all who sought it.

He is said to have composed operas as well as many hundreds of songs. He composed more new ragas than any other Indian composer. During his lifetime he had twenty pupils, through whom his songs have been promulgated through the generations. This of course was long before the day of the mechanical recording of music. Hence our knowledge of his songs and of the correctness of the original versions, depends entirely upon the accuracy with which they have been transmitted orally. Later on these beautiful melodies,which had been handed down orally, were recorded in Indian musical notation. But they still have to be learned orally from competent Indian musicians.

Three other noted musicians of this period should be mentioned. They are Gopal Krishna Bharati, Vedanayagam Sastriar, and M. Abraham Pandithar.

Gopal Krishna Bharati was a contemporary of Tyagaraja and was on friendly terms with him. He could both sing and compose music. He was one of the greatest of the composers. He is most of all famed for the literary production called "Nandinar Charitram", which he wrote in Tamil and published in 1861. It is a collection of songs based upon the story of a pious Harijan (untouchable) who, as a reward for his devotion to Siva was granted a vision of the deity in the temple at Chidambaram.

Vedanayagam Sastriar of Tanjore (1774-1864) was both a noted singer and a prolific composer of hymns in Tamil for use in the Christian Church. Many of these have been published in hymnals and are in common use. His name is held in high reputation in the Tamil churches.

M. Abraham Pandithar (1859-1919) is reputed as the author of a large two-volume work in Tamil, containing much valuable information about the music of the ancient Tamil people. He took part in the first All-India Music Conference at Baroda in 1916 and was honored by the Government of India with the title of Rao Sahib. *

Another poet-musician (1862-1919) who deserves special mention is Narayan Vaman Tilak. He was born of Brahman parentage in

* means literally Brahman gentleman, equivalent to English Lord.

Western India in the Maratha country. He became a baptized Christian in 1895. The Maratha churches are forever indebted to him for the many beautiful hymns which he composed.

From the last decade of the nineteenth century the classical music entered a new phase. Formerly such music had been generally performed by artists in private homes. Later the era of the public concert (Sangita Sabha) began. These concerts were patronized by the rajahs and the rich. From the 1930's, even before attaining political independence, India was entering a period of musical renaissance. With the coming of the radio, the record-player and the moving-picture show, the fortunes of Indian music have been rapidly changing. There has been a great increase in popularity of simple film tunes. This might indicate that classical music is on the wane. However, twenty years ago in North India, people usually requested to have good music played only on some special occasion. Now, thanks to the efforts of the All-India Radio, steps have been taken to broadcast the playing and singing of selections which illustrate the best traditions of classical music. The music used in moving-picture shows has also improved.

Moreover, concerts are now periodically held in such centers as Bombay, Poona, Delhi, Calcutta and Madras, which foster the performance of classical Indian music, as well as drama and folk music. In Madras there is a Music Academy, which has held an annual series of concerts since the year 1926. These concerts are held about ten successive days at Christmas time. During the daytime the Academy holds meetings at which special papers are read and discussed by experts and prizes are awarded to competitive singers. In the evenings concerts are given by some of the finest artists from all over India.

Provision has also been made in some Indian universities for special instruction in Indian music. In Madras, since the year 1944 in the Kala-Kshetra school, and in the Central College of Carnatic Music from the year 1949, instruction in music is now being given under the management of Mrs. Rukmani Devi. The University of Madras teaches the theory and performance of Indian music. It also conducts annual examinations and certificates are awarded to the successful candidates. At the college of Chidambaram there is a regular course leading to a degree in music. In 1956 Mrs. Indira Gandhi, now Prime Minister of India, inaugurated a new university at Khairagarh, North India, which was estimated to cost two million rupees and possesses teaching personnel in music, the dance, and the fine arts.

CHAPTER III

THE INDIAN SCALE AND THE DRONE CHORD

In order to appreciate India's music, one should have a clear understanding of its fundamental characteristics, governing rules, and the effective procedures. These subjects are treated only in brief outline in this chapter. The student should remind himself that the fundamentals of all music are three: Melody, Harmony and Rhythm. Except for the drone-chord, Harmony, as known in the West, does not exist in Indian music; whereas Melody and Rhythm are highly developed and have been set forth in definite systems. Melody will be considered in more detail in Chapter IV and Rhythm in Chapter V.

Let us now note some of the typical differences between Western and Indian music.

1. **Tone Quality.** In the West great importance is attached to quality of tone. The aim is to produce a tone which will be free from harshness and from nasal or chest qualities and which will be pleasing to the ear. In Indian music, on the other hand, the emphasis is not so much upon quality as upon accuracy of pitch and dexterity in the production of tones. This involves those subtle changes in pitch which have been improperly called "quarter tones". In India there has been a relative indifference to the presence in a singer, for example, of a loud, harsh, or even nasal tone, and an admiration for the musician who skilfully produces all the characteristic tones of a raga (See Chapter IV). An Indian singer uses his voice as a kind of musical instrument. He may produce a succession of tones with great rapidity and precision. On the other hand, it must not be inferred that there is no good quality of tone in Indian singers. One does hear frequently good tone quality in singers of classical music, but it remains true that the main excellence of such performances does not lie in their tone quality.

2. **Melody.** Western music is essentially harmony-based. That is to say, the melody is generally accompanied by one or more "parts", such as alto, tenor and bass. This harmony may vary from note to note of the melody. In Indian music, however, this is not so: the melody is

15

either carried by a soloist or by a group of performers singing or playing in unison, with the accompaniment of a single, sustained Drone-Chord. Or, instead of a chord, it may be simply the sustained key-note (the tonic) of the piece being performed. This key-note is called *sruti* in Indian music. The term "sruti" has also another meaning, which will be indicated later. The "drone-chord" consists of three notes in the key in which the piece is being performed: the two octaves with the Fifth in between. In the key of C this will be C G Č. In Indian notation this is Sa Pa Sa. The drone-chord is usually sounded on a four-stringed instrument called the *Tambura,* or upon a small accordionlike organ called a Harmonium. This chord must sound softly but continuously throughout the performance of a particular selection of music. It is therefore the background of the melody.

Mr. C. S. Ayyar, an eminent Indian musicologist, has written on this subject.

There have been two musical events in history which have · resulted in the production of certain structural changes in Carnatic music. One is the "drone-chord", which probably arose (in India) soon after the days of Rama Matya (1550 A.D.).

The presence of the drone-chord in Indian music is probably one reason why the music may sound monotonous to the listener's ear at the first hearing. Failure to grasp the importance of the drone-chord may cause musicians who are accustomed to Western harmonies to introduce such harmonic accompaniments into whatever Indian melody they are playing. The result may sound agreeable but it is *not* Indian music.

3. **Rhythm** (Tala). Indian music has many kinds of rhythm. These will be described more fully in Chapter V. Here it is necessary to point the student to some general characteristics. In classical music especially, rhythm is quite elaborate and complicated. During a concert an expert drummer often will delight his audience by executing the most intricate and fascinating rhythmic patterns. These patterns, of course, are all contained within the steady main beat of the performance. (See Chapter V)

Another point to remember is that the Indian *tempo* differs considerably from the Western. In Indian classical music there are three forms: *slow, medium,* and *fast.* The medium tempo is just twice as fast as the slow, and the fast tempo is just twice as fast as the medium. Since classical music generally involves long stretches of musical notes and syllables which have to be encompassed within the main beat, the selection begins in the slow tempo, and may move later to the higher speed. Now we come to an important contrast. In Western music the tempo may suddenly quicken in pace, or slow down, or even come to a full stop. Popular Indian music frequently changes its tempo. This is not true of South Indian (Carnatic) classical music which, excepting for the three speeds of *slow, moderate* and *fast,* continues evenly and without pause

16

until the end of the selection which is being performed. Consequently, if a singer, for example, fails to begin the line of his song at the beginning of the measure he must wait until the Number One Beat comes around again before joining in. It is necessary that the student remember this very important fact about Indian rhythm.

4. The **Scale.** This is a fundamental of Indian music. It is the basis of its elaborate melodies. A careful study of it will greatly aid the student to understand what will be said about the Raga in Chapter IV. At this point the author must be pardoned for introducing material which will be elementary to most musicians. This is done in order to help the student to a clearer understanding of India's music.

Let us first consider what in the West is called the "tempered scale", to which all pianos and organs are tuned. Take the middle "C" on the piano and play up an octave on all the *white* keys. Note the illustration below. Under each Western key letter is written the Indian *sol-fa,* using the terminology, Sa-Ri-Ga. *It is important that, from the very beginning, the student be thoroughly familiar with this terminology.* A dot over one of these symbols indicates the octave above, and a dot underneath indicates the octave below..

C	D	E	F	G	A	B	Ċ
Sa	Ri	Ga	Ma	Pa	Da	Ni	Sa

In the "tempered scale" there are 12 semitones. Seven of these are given in the above example. The remaining five semitones are found by playing the following black keys on the piano. Note that the Indian corresponding symbols are given without capital letters.

Db	Eb	F#	Ab	Bb
ri	ga	ma	da	ni

These five notes in the Key of C are, respectively, D-Flat, E-Flat, F-Sharp, A-Flat, and B-Flat. (See section on the Scale, Appendix) The 12 semitones are called "the chromatic scale".

We should now note the differences between the so-called 'tempered scale' and the 'just scale'. The tempered scale was developed in the West in medieval times to make possible the playing of harmonies upon the piano and pipe organ. In all musical scales, Eastern or Western, it should be observed that each tone, or note, has a particular number of tone vibrations per second. (See Appendix) In the case of octaves, this means that a tone which is an octave higher than the tone below it, will have just twice as many tone vibrations. In the case of the tempered scale the intermediate tones have been adjusted so that one proceeds up the scale of 12 semi-tones by increasing the tone-vibrations per second by the same number in each case. In the Indian just scale, however, this increase is not equal. The number of tone-vibrations for each note will

17

vary. The Indian scale is harmonically truer than the Western. If a particular note is not played at its true position, the resulting clash of vibrations is called "beats". This is true for the 12 semitones of the Western scale. In addition, the Indian scale includes ten more microtones (srutis), making a total of 22. (See Appendix). Some of these 22 microtones are so close to their neighboring tones as to be almost indistinguishable except to a good musical ear. About this Mr. C. S. Ayyar has written:

> "the extra ten microtones of the Indian scale may be said to be small variations of the ratio frequencies of those notes, which, other than *Sa* (C) and *Pa* (G) can be achieved on the ten frets of the *Vina.*" (See Chapter VI).

Students who are interested in the physics and mathematics of this subject are advised to pursue it in one of the books listed in the bibliography, such as Sir James Jeans' *Science and Music,* or C. S. Ayyar's *The Grammar of South Indian Music.*

The "just intonation" of the Indian scale, therefore, means that, excepting for the notes of the chord C-G-C (Sa-Pa-Sa), which are fixed according to the laws of harmony, all other of the 22 microtones are *not* tonally equidistant from each other, but bear certain ratio-frequencies with reference to the tonic *Sa.* In the drone chord (Sa-Pa-Sa) the Fifth (Pa) is in perfect harmony with the tonic Sa. In other words, the Pa of the Indian scale is a perfect Fifth, which is not true in the tempered scale. Similarly the Fourth (Ma) of the Indian scale is a true Fourth. In the tempered scale the Fifth is slightly lower, and the Fourth slightly higher, than they should be, according to just intonation. It would be very difficult to construct a piano which would have all the 22 microtones of the Indian scale!

All these tonal differences may seem very slight to the student, but they do exist. Every good musician is aware of this. Observe, for example, how a western violinist tunes his instrument of four strings. These strings are (proceeding upward from the lowest string): G, D, A, and E. Every violinist will tune these strings in pairs of Fifths. That is, D is a perfect Fifth with G, and in the same way A with D, and E with A. On the piano these are not perfect Fifths but on the violin they *must* be so. Likewise every good violinist knows that the note G-Sharp and the note A-Flat just above it are not one and the same. He achieves the one or the other tone by sliding his finger up or down the pertinent string just a little. But on the piano these are combined in one key.

These illustrations should help the student understand and appreciate the Indian scale. In the course of time he should become able to detect with his ear most of the 22 microtones.

Professor P. Sambamoorthy has written: "Music is an exact science. The notes of the musical systems of all countries will bear recognized ratios to the fundamental notes." * The philosopher George Santayana has written that music is a rationalization of sound and mathematics become audible.

From the foregoing the reader may now better understand the significance of the drone chord in India's music. There seems to be nothing remotely like it in Western music, classical or popular. In the extreme forms of current popular music known as jazz or rock 'n' roll continuous rhythmic chords are repeated in succession, over and over again. There may be two or three of these chords which are played upon the guitar or other stringed instruments, continuously, but never just one chord. In India's classical music all melodies depend upon this continuously sounding harmonic base. The usual instrument for the drone-chord is the Tambura. (See Chapter VI.) At the beginning of a performance the singer or instrumental soloist will carefully fix the pitch of this chord. Each classical song usually runs into two octaves. Unless the singer has an extraordinary wide vocal range, he will probably prefer to set his basal tonic (Sa) fairly low — for example, either at C or at C-Sharp. Having the Tambura, he can dispense with a piano pitch and tune it to suit his voice. The singer will take much pains at the beginning of his concert to oversee the tuning of the Tambura and to test it at intervals, much as a Western violinist will occasionally retune his violin during a performance, in order to have perfect pitch. Sometimes, in the case of a song of a more popular type, if the pitch seems too low, it may be desirable to shift the tonic pitch to the Fourth above. This means that the Fourth (Ma) will become the new Sa, and the upper Sa becomes the new Fifth (Pa). In this way the drummer will not be required to change the pitch of his drumhead — a matter which would considerably delay the performance. (See Chapter VI).

When the student listens for the first time to Indian music of the classical type, the sound of the drone-chord, as we have already noted, may seem a bit monotonous to him because he is paying too much attention to it. He may find it difficult to dissociate his attention from the chord in order to enjoy the melodic excellence of the selection being rendered. For him to pass an immediate adverse judgment upon the music at that point because of such monotony would be like the case of a person who was witnessing his first baseball game and found the presence of the "home-plate" too monotonous! The vast majority of the spectators are watching the progress of the ball-game. They watch the ball as it leaves the pitcher, the batter as he hits the ball, and the fielders as they field it. Nobody is looking at the home-plate. But if the home-plate is not where it is expected to be, there certainly would be no ball-game.

It is the same way with a concert of classical Indian music. One who listens to it fairly will enjoy immensely the melody and rhythm.

* Sambamoorthy, SOUTH INDIAN MUSIC, Book V, p. 1.

Both of these features can be very complex and distinctive. Although the drone chord is continuously sounding softly, he does not fix his attention primarily upon it. It is to the combination of the melody, with its witchery of subtle tones, and to the fascinatingly complex drum rhythm against the tonal background of the Tambura, that he gives his delighted attention.

CHAPTER IV

RAGA: THE SOUL OF INDIAN MUSIC

Rabindranath Tagore, the famous Nobel prize-winning poet of Bengal, has written the following significant words:

> For us, music has above all a transcendental significance. It disengages the spiritual from the happenings of life; it sings of the relationships of the human soul with the soul of things beyond. The world by day is like European music; a flowing concourse of vast harmony, composed of concord and discord and many disconnected fragments. And the night world is our Indian music; one pure, deep and tender raga. They both stir us, yet the two are contradictory in spirit. But that cannot be helped. At the very root nature is divided into two, day and night, unity and variety, finite and infinite. We men of India live in the realm of night; we are overpowered by the sense of the One and Infinite. Our music draws the listener away beyond the limits of everyday human joys and sorrows, and takes us to that lonely region of renunciation which lies at the root of the universe, while European music leads us a variegated dance through the endless rise and fall of human grief and joy. *

From this one can discern that Raga is the very soul of India's music. Professor P. Sambamoorthy, who is also well acquainted with Western music, has written, "Raga is the pivotal concept of Indian music . . . . . The ideal of absolute music is reached in the concept of the Raga. The whole structure of Indian music is built around (it)." *

It is therefore vitally important at the outset of one's study to have a clear understanding of the term. Like every human being, each raga has its own individual name and characteristics. Every Indian song is

* Popley, MUSIC OF INDIA, p. 132.

* Sambamoorthy, SOUTH INDIAN MUSIC, Book II, p. 1.

usually built upon some raga, and all classical music must be based upon a raga. The term means, literally, *mood* or *passion*. This aspect of the word will be taken up presently.

Raga has also been roughly defined as a *melody-scale* or *melody-type*. In Western music a "scale" means a succession of the seven main notes, or of the 12 chromatic notes, which lie within an octave. As observed in an earlier chapter, the Western scale, using the key of C, runs as follows, with its corresponding *sol-fa* notes in both Western and Indian nomenclature:

C	D	E	F	G	A	B	Ċ
Doh	Re	Mi	Fa	Sol	La	Ti	Ḋoh
Sa	Ri	Ga	Ma	Pa	Da	Ni	Ṡa

It is important, from the very start, to become thoroughly familiar with the Indian Sa-Ri-Ga. (See Appendix).

As already stated, the Indian scale has a total of at least 22 microtones. One musicologist has asserted that there may be as many as 34. Each of the 22 has its individual name and ratio frequency of tone with respect to the tonic, or basal *Sa*.

It must be borne in mind that the term "scale" is not an accurate description of a *raga*. A raga is a combination of musical phrases, shapes and contours which give a characteristic melodic identity in a way that the term "scale" cannot give. It is a succession of tones, or notes, which bear a relationship to the basal pitch (Sa) of the drone-chord. Each raga has its individual name and characteristic ascending (Arohana) and descending (Avarohana) notes.

There are legends about the origin of the ragas. One is that in ancient times there were five ragas, which were composed by famous rishis or musicians. Later musicians composed and added more to the original stock. Just how many ragas there are is not known. One authority states that there are 120,000! Others say the number is limitless. But it is well known that today there are at least 250 ragas in common use in South Indian music.

Historically, various attempts have been made to classify the ragas. The oldest theory held that all ragas were divided into three groups, *Ragas, Raginis* (wife-ragas), and *Puttiras* (son-ragas). This theory was found useless and was discarded.

As already noted, by the end of the fourteenth century, India's classical music became divided into two schools, the Northern (Hindustani) and the Southern (Carnatic). Each school developed its own rules, and musical systems. There is, therefore, no one standard for all India. This applies especially to the Ragas. Each school, while not unlike the other in some respects, has pursued a more or less independent course. As a result one often finds the same raga in both schools but under a different name, and with different characteristic notes. Or, under the same raga name the notes will differ. Still further, certain ragas may exist in one school but not in the other. The terminology for notes in the scale differs somewhat as between the two schools. (See Appendix). One Indian musicologist has pleaded for a common system of nomenclature, in order that the adherents of each school may become familiar with the individual resemblances and differences between them.

A second method of classification, as developed in the Southern School, is the division into two classes, called *Primary,* or parent, and *Secondary,* or derivative, ragas. This classification is really very useful. There are in all 72 Primary ragas. Each contains all seven notes of the scale. They differ from one another by the use of sharps or flats in the scale. The first 36 of the Primary ragas always have the natural Fourth note and the other 36, the sharpened Fourth. A Secondary raga usually may not have all the main notes of its Primary, or parent, raga. It may be pentatonic or hexatonic, or it may have other variations.

A third method of classification is by the characteristic *time of day or night* when the raga may be used. Both the Northern and Southern Schools follow this method.

Some authorities have divided the day into the following periods: from 4 to 7 a.m.; 10 a.m. to 12 noon; 1 to 4 p.m.; 4 p.m. to evening; 7 to 10 p.m.; and 10 p.m. till midnight. Others report the divisions of the day differently. In general, ragas may be grouped into those which may be sung in the morning, during the afternoon or evening, and at night. Many ragas may be sung at any time of day or night. However, some ragas lend themselves peculiarly to use in the morning. others to use at night only. Although these classifications are still important, they are not now so rigidly adhered to as formerly. Nowadays if a musician happens to sing or play a raga at an inauspicious time of day, at the close of his performance he will probably play or sing a final selection in a particularly auspicious raga. This, it is assumed, will appease the deity who presides over music. Mr. Sambamoorthy has written about the subject.

The time theory of ragas is based on the principle that the ragas sound best when sung or performed during the allotted time. The rule is however *not* of a mandatory nature, but of an *advisory* character. The fact that when a king (rajah) asks for a raga, a vidwan (musical artist) can sing it irrespective of the time or season during which it should be sung, shows that the rule relating to the time for singing a raga is not an inviolable one. *

According to another Indian musicologist the real cause for such rules regarding time of day is probably a physiological one. For example,

* Sambamoorthy, SOUTH INDIAN MUSIC, Book III, p. 21.

the singing of the raga *Maya-malava-goula* in the morning, and of *Kalyani* in the evening, seems to come more naturally and easily to the human voice.

A fourth method of classification is to group the ragas according to the particular *mood, passion* or *feeling* evoked. Both Schools observe this distinction. The authorities list as many as nine different emotions, or moods, any one of which may be indicated in an individual raga. These emotions are: joy, sorrow, anger, laughter, pity, love, fear, tenderness, and tranquillity. The emotion of *bhakti* is really a complex of faith, love and devotion. Mr. Sambamoorthy classifies all ragas under three heads: (1) those which can arouse any of the emotions, (2) those which create pure aesthetic joy, and (3) those which can create both aesthetic joy and any one of the emotions at the same time. This indicates that classical music is often enjoyed because of the beauty of its sound and structure and not necessarily because it evokes a particular mood or emotion. It might be fair to say that the presence of two or more flattened notes of the scale conduces in the listener a feeling of pathos. Conversely, the use of what may be called a *major* scale, or mode, tends to create a feeling of joy. On the other hand, the ability of a musician to create certain feelings in the breast of his listeners by his music may depend upon a number of other factors, such as the *tempo* employed, or certain mannerisms, or gestures.

Ragas are said to be able to cause not only emotions but certain physical effects. For example, the snake-charmer claims to attract or control the cobra by playing a certain raga on his pipe. Although a snake does not have ears, it is in some way affected by the music. The use of the raga *Bilahari* is believed by Indian musicians to be helpful in reducing body pains and promoting health. (See Appendix). There is also a raga which is said to cause fire, and another which will cause rain. India with its periodic droughts, might perhaps benefit greatly by the use of this raga!

There is an interesting story about the Fire Raga. A certain king had at his court a famous musician. One day the king heard about this raga and ordered the musician to demonstrate his powers with it. He commanded the musician to descend into the Jumna River, stand in the water up to his neck, and then to intone the Fire Raga. As he did so, flames burst from his neck and consumed him! Another legend adds that a musician friend then sang the Rain Raga, which quenched the flames and saved the court musician. Whatever historical facts underlie these lengends, this certainly illustrates the popular belief in the power of music to work unusual effects.

We are familiar with the story of the Hebrew musician David, who by his singing and harp-playing was able to soothe the melancholy and troubled spirit of King Saul. There are also Indian legends which tell how the famous shepherd-musician Krishna could cast a spell over men and animals by his marvellous playing upon the flute.

24

At this point the reader is cautioned to keep in mind a very important fact about the raga. The ability to sing or to play the characteristic notes of a raga does not necessarily mean that he has mastered the raga itself. A raga is something more than its characteristic notes. What is that "something"? In Indian terms it is called the *raga-bhava,* or the life of the raga. It is not easy to explain this in a book. It has to be demonstrated by an expert singer or player. When the expert demonstrates a raga by voice or instrument, he brings it to life both to himself and to his hearers. The effect is usually produced by the use of gamakas (grace notes or embellishments).

There are 15 or more kinds of embellishments. They are embodied in a series of vocal exercises which the student should practise until he attains mastery. Most of the ragas are to be practised in vocal exercises called "varnas". These bring out all the characteristic notes and phrases of the particular raga. Some of these exercises are given in books but they can be learned properly only under a good teacher. The expert can reproduce these embellishments with his voice or instrument. Some of them resemble a kind of *glissando,* or a slurring from one tone to another adjacent in pitch in such a way as to convey to the ear certain intervening microtones *(srutis).* Excepting the octaves and fifth in between, *many* or *all* of the *notes* (swaras) of a *raga* may be thus *slurred,* or *shaken.* But the drone-chord (Sa-Pa-Sa) may not be shaken in performance, but must remain constant in pitch.

It is this kind of singing or playing, against the background of the *drone,* which constitutes the chief beauty of Indian classical music. Western melodies are produced to the accompaniment of constantly changing harmonies: whereas in Indian music the variations are produced by the grace notes or other melodic phrasings. The lack of that kind of phrasing in Western music is one reason why Indian musicians do not generally appreciate Western music. The latter seems to them too plain and unvarnished, or like a cake without flavor or frosting. It is the presence of these vocal or instrumental tone embellishments, however, which make it very difficult to record the full beauty of Indian classical music in staff notation.

A word may be added about the seating arrangement of musicians in a typical concert of classical Indian music. The performers are seated on the floor of a platform, with the solo singer or solo instrumentalist seated in the center and the others around him. The Tambura (or drone instrument) player will sit behind and to one side of the soloist. The drummer sits at the right of the soloist and the violin or other supporting instrument at his left, both players partly facing the soloist.

At the beginning of a musical selection, the soloist and the violinist will perform what is called the *Alapana (Alap).* This consists of a kind of warm-up, or vivifying, of the particular raga on which the solo is based. There is no rhythm at first, the drummer remaining silent, but the drone-chord will be sounding. The soloist will intone a certain phrase or phrases in the raga. As soon as he finishes, the violinist will take up, repeat, and work over the same phrases. This is continued until the soloist and the accompanying violinist have worked out the characteristic phrases of the raga in all its windings, thus giving it full life. The process may be brief, or it may take 20 or more minutes depending upon the skill of the performers. After this introductory Alapana is finished, the song proper with rhythmic accompaniment begins. The drummer joins in with all the rhythmic skill of which he is capable. Occasionally a classical song may begin without the Alapana, but this is not usual in concerts.

Another feature of a concert should also be noted. The soloist is permitted to do one or both of two things. He may sing the particular song just as its composer intended it to be sung, but he usually adds his own improvisations. Whatever he does, he must adhere strictly to the characteristic notes of the raga on which his song is based. Of this Mr. Sambamoorthy writes, "In a concert (of classical music) we have not only the composition of a great composer but also the performer's creative music — music improvised and presented on the spot." * It is this fact of improvisation which Mr. Beverly Nichols, in a chapter of his book, VERDICT ON INDIA, p. 149, seems not to have appreciated. Nichols referred to his unsuccessful attempt to induce an Indian professional singer to repeat a line of a classical song, in order that Mr. Nichols might record it in staff notation. Because the singer sang the same line with different variations each time, Nichols finally gave up in disgust. It is a great pity that he became so easily discouraged and hence has created a false impression about Indian music in his book.

Finally, a word must be said about notation. Through staff notation Western musicians have made a great contribution to the cause of transcribing musical compositions. As a result, any person with the requisite musical training can reproduce the music of the great masters as it was intended to be reproduced. In a similar fashion Indian musicians in modern times have tried to record their musical masterpieces in some form or other of Indian notation, such as Sanskrit, Telegu, or Tamil script. But the difficulties of recording such music in any form are very great. This is especially true of staff notation. The author of this book, in Chapter IX, has made an attempt in this way to convey to the westerner some idea of the beauties of Carnatic music. But it must be reiterated that the result gives only the bare bones of the original. They must be sung by an expert to bring out the *raga bhava* (the life) of the song thus notated. Some Indian musicologists have pleaded for the use of Indian notation only, claiming that it is sufficient for all purposes. They declaim against the use of staff notation for their music.

* Sambamoorthy, SOUTH INDIAN MUSIC, Book II, p. 2.

26

In order to illustrate this subject further, the following six Carnatic ragas are given below in some detail. The underlined notes are to be shaken.

It is customary for the beginner when practising the ascending and descending characteristics of a raga first to perform it at a slow tempo as if the notes were whole notes. He then repeats the exercise in double the tempo as if using half nótes. Next he doubles that speed, and continues doubling the speed until he has reached the limit at which he can perform.

Separate lists of both Hindustani and Carnatic ragas are given in the Appendix. Some essential data is given in the case of each raga, such as its characteristic notes in staff notation and, wherever possible, the name by which it is called in the other School. (See Appendix.)

Maya-malava-gaula ⤙ Primary 15 (Bhairava). Morning: reverence.

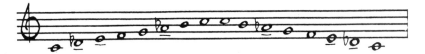

This is one of the oldest ragas in South Indian music. It is said to have originated in the middle face of the five faces of the god Mahadeva (Siva). Note that it consists of a series of pairs of microtones. Music teachers in South India give the first lessons to their pupils in this raga.

Sankarabharana — Primary 29 (Bilaval). 10 a.m. to 2 p.m. Calm.

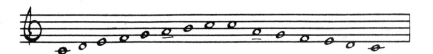

This is one of the easiest ragas for Western musicians, for it resembles the "tempered scale". This may come as a surprise to those persons who have imagined that all Oriental music is in a minor key. Although it is primarily a morning raga, it may be used at any hour of the day. In it the Sixth and Seventh notes (Da and Ni) are slightly sharpened, and the Seventh (Ni) is sometimes omitted in the descending characteristics (Avarohana).

27

Thodi — Secondary from Primary 8 (Bhairavi). Night to 6 a.m., sadness, majesty

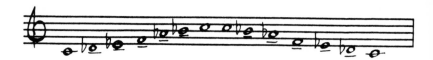

This raga differs from its parent raga in that the Fifth (Pa) is generally omitted. If played in the key of C on the piano, it will be noted that all the black keys of the scale are played. It is much like the chromatic scale. It is peculiarly suitable for training singers to do vocal exercises in the ragas. Most of the notes are shaken except Sa Pa S̈a.

Hamsa Dwani — Secondary from Primary 29. Any time of day: songs of love and devotion.

This is a very popular and beautiful pentatonic raga. In it the Fourth (Ma) and the Sixth (Da) are omitted. Many songs have been composed in it, one of which is a brilliant hymn of praise to the elephant-headed god Ganapathi (Ganesh) by the musician Dikshitar. (See Chapters II & IX).

Mohana — Secondary from Primary 28 (Bhupathi). Any time, sweetness, joy.

This is one of the oldest modes in the world. It is a pentatonic raga, in that the Fourth (Ma) and the Seventh (Ni) are omitted. The melody of the old song, "There Is a Happy Land, Far, Far Away" is in this raga. The melody undoubtedly originated in India.

Kalyani — Secondary from Primary 65.   Evening: merriment.

The main difference between this raga and Sankarabharana is that the Fourth (Ma) is sharpened. As in the case of Thodi raga, the Fifth (Pa) is traditionally omitted from use, but this is not now observed in practice. This raga is also useful for vocalizing exercises in ragas.

CHAPTER V.

TALA (RHYTHM)

Whatever may be one's reaction to Indian music as a whole, it is difficult to understand how he could fail to be attracted to its intricate and fascinating rhythms. Most people instinctively appreciate rhythm, especially if they have learned to dance or to keep time. Folk and popular music have a great deal of rhythm. In the West new types of popular music have arisen, such as jazz and swing, and, more recently rock 'n' roll. Many of these rhythms originated from African music. They fascinate many, particularly young people. The "Beatles" have greatly promoted this type of music. It has much syncopation and is exceedingly rhythmic. The musicians who play this music have the ability to improvise the melody, harmony and the rhythm of such music "on the spot". Furthermore, through the interest and influence of George Harrison, one of the Beatles, there is a growing interest in the melodies and rhythms of India's classical music on the part of many of the young people in the West today. Witness the great popularity of the music of the Indian **sitar** player, Ravi Shankar.

The beauty of Indian rhythms can be realized in a special way by listening to expert Indian drummers in a public concert of classical music. (See Chapter VI for description of the drum.) Although there is good drumming among Western musicians, there is nothing quite so impressive as the Indian drumming.

One good way to acquire this appreciation is to visit India and listen to the drummer at a concert. Or, if one happens to be on tour of India and halts for the night near a village where some social function is going on, such as a wedding or a funeral, he can hear drumming in the neighborhood. If he happens to lie awake in bed unable to sleep, he may find it fun to see how many changes in rhythmic patterns take place within a very short time. He is likely to be amazed at the number of changes. It can be a fascinating pastime.

When, however, one turns from popular to classical music, one comes to realize the force of Mr. Sambamoorthy's words, "The tala (Rhythm) system is perhaps the most difficult and complicated branch of South Indian music". *

Such rhythms may be described as *diversity within unity*.

The place of the drummer in classical music is very important. In every public concert it is customary for the soloist on occasion to give the drummer an opportunity to display his individual skill. The soloist at any desirable point will break off from singing. Meanwhile the drone-chord is continuously sounding and the tala proceeds without pause. This is the signal for the drummer to take over. At once he will redouble his efforts and "go all out" to impress the audience with a perfect whirlwind of cross-beats and embroidery on the main rhythm which will thrill his hearers. After some minutes of this the soloist will resume his song, by beginning a line of a stanza at Beat Number One of a particular measure. At that point the drummer with a flourish, stops the cross-beats, without missing a beat, takes up the regular rhythm with the soloist, and they continue together while the audience bursts into wild applause. It is a triumph of skill on the part of the drummer.

As in the case of Raga, the Northern and Southern Schools treat the subject of Tala somewhat differently. Many of the terms are the same but the names and methods of classification may be different. In this chapter the subject is treated from the viewpoint of the Southern School. According to tradition there are over 100 different varieties of rhythm. But the ordinary number given is 35. (See Appendix). Many of these are known only to pedants and to expert professional musicians. We consider here only five which are in common use, both in classical and popular music. Before doing so, it is necessary to explain some essential parts of Indian rhythms.

Each measure, or time-bar (Avarta) is composed of a total of from 3 to 8 or even 22 time-units. These are called *Aksharas*. Each measure is composed of one or more time-members (Angas), each time-member having a certain number of time-units. There are three kinds of time-members: *Druta, Anudruta* and *Laghu*. A measure will contain one or more of these.

1. *Druta.* This has two time-units. These are indicated by (first) a handclap and (second) by a handwave.

2. *Anudruta.* This has only one time-unit and is indicated by a single handclap.

3. *Laghu.* This generally comes first in the measure (Avarta). It will contain a total of 3, 4, 5, 7 or 9 time-units. The first time-unit will be indicated by a handclap (See Table of Talas, Appendix), and the

* Sambamoorthy, SOUTH INDIAN MUSIC, Book II, p. 13.

32

remaining time-units are indicated by a series of finger-counts of one hand, beginning with the little finger, which is struck against the thigh or the palm of the other hand.

We may take, for example, the rhythm of eight time-units called Triputa Tala Chatusra Jati. This is popularly called *Adi Tala*. Its signature is 4:2:2, or four plus two plus two equals eight time-units. It is used in both classical and popular music. The word "chatusra" means "four". It means in this instance that the Laghu, which begins the measure, has 4 time-units. The measure can be expressed as follows:

Time-unit No. 1. A handclap (Laghu).
No. 2. One beat of the little finger.
No. 3. One beat by the finger next to the little finger.
No. 4. One beat by the middle finger.
No. 5. A handclap (Druta).
No. 6. A handwave.
No. 7. A handclap (Druta).
No. 8. A handwave.

Each time-unit succeeds the one before it with absolute regularity. The only stress, or accent, comes on the handclap. This is indicated in the following diagram, showing the whole measure with its eight time-units, or beats, each stressed beat, or handclap, indicated by the mark "X" above it, and each handwave indicated by "U".

```
X         X U X U   X         X U X U
1  2  3  4 5 6 7 8   1  2  3  4 5 6 7 8
```

Or, one may group these eight beats into two multiples of four each and put the stress over the first three beats, and indicate beat No. 4 in each case by the mark "U" thus:

```
X X X U   X X X U
1 2 3 4   1 2 3 4
```

Three handclaps and one handwave. The handclaps can also be demonstrated by cymbals or castanets.

2. *Rupaka Tala Chatusra Jati*. This is commonly called "*Rupaka Tala*". Its rhythm differs from that of Adi Tala in that the measure has a total of six time-units, or beats, instead of eight. It is made up of two time-members: one Druta followed by one Laghu of 4 time-units. Its signature is 2:4, or 2 beats plus 4 beats equals six beats. It can be set forth as follows:

Time-unit No. 1. A handclap. (Druta)
No. 2. A handwave.
No. 3. A handclap. (Laghu)
No. 4. Beat by little finger.

33

No. 5. Beat by finger next to little finger.
No. 6. Beat by middle finger.
This can be illustrated as follows:

```
X  U  X              X  U  X
1  2  3  4  5  6      1  2  3  4  5  6
```

However, it is more usual to maintain the beat differently, as follows: The stress comes on Beat Number One and Three as usual but Beat Numbers Five and Six are included in one handwave.

```
X     X     (Wave)   X     X     (Wave)
1  2  3  4  5  6      1  2  3  4  5  6
```

At this point it should be noted that, wherever the finger count is dispensed with in this way, the Tala may also be called "Chapu Tala", although this title usually refers to the Tala which we next describe.

3. *Triputa Tala Trisra Jati.* This is commonly called "Chapu Tala". Its "Trisra" means "three". Its signature is 3:2:2, or 3 plus 2 plus 2 equals 7. This is a harder rhythm for a Westerner to master than either of the foregoing two Talas. It consists of a Laghu with three time-units and two Drutas. The stresses occur on time-unit Numbers One, Four and Six. Thus

```
X        X    X       X        X    X
1  2  3  4  5  6  7    1  2  3  4  5  6  7
```

It is more commonly shown, however, by two handclaps only, and with no fingercounts, or handwaves, thus:

```
X        X            X        X
1  2  3  4  5  6  7    1  2  3  4  5  6  7
```

Instead of a handclap, the stresses may be shown, as in the case of other rhythms, by cymbals or castanets.

4. *Jampai Tala Misra Jati.* "Misra" means "seven". The signature is 7:1:2 or 7 plus 1 plus 2 equals 10. This is called "Jampai Tala". It is also a rather difficult Tala to master. Usually the ten time-units are divided in two groups of five time-units each, so that the measure has a total of five beats, with the stress coming on Beat Numbers One, Three and Four. No handwave or fingercount.

```
X     X  X       X     X  X
1  2  3  4  5     1  2  3  4  5
```

34

5. *Eka Tala.* This is Number One in the Table of Talas. It consists of a measure with only one time-member, namely the Laghu which may have only 3 or 4 time-units. Therefore it much resembles the 3/4 or 4/4 time of Western music and is quite easy to perform. There is only one stress, which comes on the first time-unit, or beat, of the measure.

It must be noted that in addition to the rhythms shown in the Table of Talas, the drummer uses his own patterns which are different and far more complicated. These cannot be given here but must be learned only from an expert drummer. To maintain these regular rhythms the concert drum, which is tuned, is used. But there are many other kinds of drums (not tuned) and many other kinds of percussion instruments. These will be described in detail in Chapter VI.

Tambura played by D. Srinavasa Iyengar
courtesy of Richard Riesz

CHAPTER VI.

PRESENT-DAY MUSICAL INSTRUMENTS

A list of India's musical instruments in use about eighty years ago may be found by consulting Captain Day's book, THE MUSICAL INSTRUMENTS OF SOUTHERN INDIA. H. A. Popley's book, MUSIC OF INDIA (published in 1921) contains another list. Collections of such instruments are on display in several large cities in India. A particularly interesting one is located in the Annamalai Manram at Georgetown, Madras. This chapter describes some of the more important instruments now in use.

Stringed Instruments.

1. The *Tambura*. This can be found in all parts of India in various sizes and models. It is a stringed instrument between four and five feet in length and with a sounding bowl at its lower end. The bowl is about ten inches wide and 12 inches deep. In South India the Tambura is made entirely of jacktree wood, the bowl being hollowed out of one piece. In North India the bowl is made from a hollow gourd. The larger of these gourds are said to be imported from Africa. The bridge for the strings is placed at the center of the bowl. There are four strings, all metal. There are no frets on the keyboard. The player sits cross-legged on the floor, holding it upright with the bowl resting on his lap. He plays the Tambura with his right hand, plucking with one finger the four strings each in succession from left to right. The strings are tuned as follows: G̣ C C C̣ (Low G in bass clef, the C above twice, and low C in the bass clef.)

         Pa Sa Sa Sa

Note: A letter without a dot means the note is in the middle octave. A dot above the letter signifies the octave above, while a dot below indicates a lower octave.

Little pieces of silk are placed underneath the strings and next to the bridge where the strings cross it. As a result of this when the strings are plucked, they produce a kind of twanging and buzzing sound as the

37

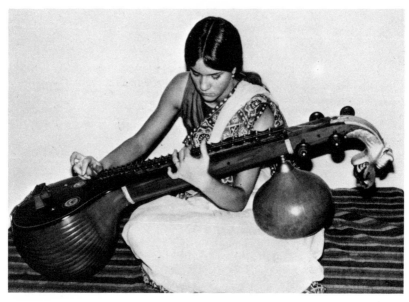

Vina played by Sarah Turcotte
courtesy of Leonard Dart

Village Band., left to right,
Nagaswara, Ottu, Dhavul

The village *Ottu* player

harmonic background of the melody. The Tambura is the ideal instrument for the Drone because of the rich harmonics of its tone. The best Tamburas are said to be made in Tanjore, South India. They are also made at the Annamalai Manram at Madras. Some of them are very beautifully ornamented. The greater degree of workmanship on a Tambura, the higher its cost. Another feature about a first class Tambura is that, by plucking its strings in certain ways, a good musical ear can detect all seven main notes of the octave at their accurate pitch. This is on the basis of harmonics.

2. The *Vina*. This is one of the oldest of India's musical instruments. It first appeared in the seventh century A.D. In shape it is somewhat similar to the Tambura, except that, in addition to the bowl at the lower end, there is also a smaller bowl at the upper end which serves as a support to the neck of the Vina. The bowl at the lower end is a hollow gourd, which serves as a resonator. The Vina has seven strings of silver or of brass. Four are "playing strings" and three sound as a drone-chord. The keyboard has 24 frets, 12 for each octave. Mr. C. S. Ayyar once wrote me that a historic musical event which has resulted in the production of certain structural changes in Carnatic music was the placing, fixed in hard wax, of the 24 frets under the four playing strings. This took place in the year 1783 as the result of the study of overtones, or harmonics. By sliding his fingers over these frets the musician produces a beautiful slurring, singing tone, and the intervening microtones can be detected. Unlike the Tambura, the Vina is usually played in a horizontal position, resting over the lap of the performer as he is seated on the floor.

There are various ways of tuning the South Indian Vina. The playing strings may be tuned thus:

$$\begin{array}{cccc} C & G & \underset{.}{C} & G \\ Sa & \underset{.}{Pa} & \dot{Sa} & \overset{..}{Pa} \end{array}$$

The drone strings will then be tuned as follows:

$$\begin{array}{ccc} G & C & \dot{G} \\ Pa & Sa & \underset{.}{Pa} \end{array}$$

3. The *Kottu Vadhyam*. This instrument resembles the Vina, except that its keyboard has no frets. Like the Vina it is played by plucking the strings with the fingers, but a small cylindrical block of wood is also used to glide over the strings in playing.

4. The *Sitar*. This is one of the most popular of North Indian instruments. It is descended from the Vina and came into existence in the 13th or 14th century during the time of the Moghul invaders. It is between three and four feet in length, and is made of teakwood. The

keyboard reminds one somewhat of the banjo, but is hollow throughout. At each end of the Sitar is a hollow gourd, which serves to amplify the sound. The keyboard has frets, which can be moved according to the raga used.

The number of strings on a Sitar varies, but usually there are 20, some of steel and some of brass. 7 of these are for playing and the rest are "sympathetic or resonating strings". The resonating strings add to the volume of the tone.

The playing strings are tuned as follows:

F	C	G	C	G	C	Ċ
Ma	Ṣa	Pa	Ṣa	Pa	Sa	Ṡa

The 13 sympathetic strings are tuned to the scale of the raga in the following succession:

C	D	C	D	E	E	F	F	G	G	A	B	Ċ
Sa	Ri	Sa	Ri	Ga	Ga	Ma	Ma	Pa	Pa	Da	Ni	Ṡa

The player plucks the playing strings with a steel wire plectrum attached to the middle finger of the right hand, or it may be played with the fingers. When playing, the fingers of the left hand slide both horizontally and vertically, thus producing the characteristic slurring tones. There are no drone strings as in the case of the Vina.

5. The *Sarod*. This is a stringed instrument about three feet long. Its keyboard has no frets and the top of the gourd at the lower end is covered with a hide. It has 6 playing strings and 13 "rhythmic", but no drone strings. The playing strings are tuned as follows:

B	D	E	C	Ċ	Ċ
Ṇi	Ri	Ga	Sa	Ṡa	Ṡa

The rhythmic strings are tuned like those of the Sitar as follows:

C	D	C	D	E	E	F	F	G	G	A	B	Ċ
Sa	Ri	Sa	Ri	Ga	Ga	Ma	Ma	Pa	Pa	Da	Ni	Ṡa

These rhythmic strings are adjustable in pitch, according to the raga being used.

6. The *Violin*. This is essentially the same as the western violin, but differs, in that the strings are tuned at the following intervals:

C	G	Ċ	Ġ
Sa	Pa	Ṡa	Ṗa

The violin is commonly used as accompanying instrument to the solo singer in all South Indian concerts. The player will sit to the left of the singer and facing him. He sits cross-legged on the floor, resting the sound-box upon the breast and the scroll against the ankle. An expert player will repeat very skillfully all the vocal phrasings of the singer when opportunity is given to him.

7. The *Sarangi*. This instrument is peculiar to North India and has been called the "Indian Violin". It is quite small, and may have three or four playing strings, one of brass and three of gut. Underneath these main strings are 23 "sympathetic strings". There are no frets. It is played with a bow and is used in both solo and group singing.

Wind Instruments.

1. The *Flute* (Murali). This is ordinarily made of hollowed-out bamboo and has the usual sound-holes. In shape it resembles the Western flute, but has no stops or keys. It has a sweet sound, and is very popular. There are a number of outstanding flute artists in India.

2. The *Nagaswara*. This is a reed instrument resembling the oboe in appearance. It is very common in southern India. It varies from two to two-and-one-half feet in length and is conical in shape. It is made of wood or metal. Its tone is very harsh and penetrating, and is too loud to be played inside a building.

3. *Ottu*. The Nagaswara is usually accompanied by an instrument similar in appearance called the "Ottu", on which a single tone is sustained as the accompanying drone. It is very interesting to note how the Ottu player sustains his tone by letting the air in his puffed-out cheeks pass through the instrument while he is drawing a fresh breath into his lungs, giving the effect of the continuous tone of a bag-pipe.

The Nagaswara and the Ottu are commonly used in the daily religious ceremonies of worship in Hindu temples and on such public social occasions as weddings or funerals.

4. The *Shenai*. This is a double-reed, woodwind instrument used in North India. It is like the Nagaswara, and is about one and one-half feet long. It is made of wood, ending in a small brass horn. It is a reed instrument and has seven holes, played like a flute.

Drums.

The best and most musical of all Indian drums are the *Mrudanga* and *Tabla*. The former is to be found in South India, the latter in North India, although it is sometimes used in South India. The Mrudanga (Nardala) is a very ancient instrument. It is in one piece, whereas the Tabla is in two separate parts.

Tabla
courtesy of the Embassy of India, U.S.A.

Mrudanga
courtesy of the Embassy of India, U.S.A.

The *mridanga* is a barrel-shaped drum about two feet long, with a girth of about three feet in the centre. The two ends have a diameter of about nine inches each. Slight variations from these dimensions may occur in different *mridanga*. The shape of the *mridanga* reminds one of two bottomless flower pots joined at the rims. The shell of the drum is now made of wood, and is slightly larger at one end than at the other. The two heads are covered with parchment, which is tightened or loosened by leather braces enclosing small cylindrical blocks of wood, which are either pushed nearer to or further from the head which is being tuned. As the strain on the braces is increased or decreased, so the parchment head is stretched or loosened, and the pitch raised or lowered as desired. On one of these two heads is worked a mixture of manganese dust, boiled rice and tamarind juice, in order to increase the pitch of the note. This appears as a black circle, slightly raised in the centre about one-eighth of an inch. It is a permanent fixture on the drum, and the bare parchment is only left for a very small width around it. The note of this head is Sa, and it is played with the fingers of the right hand, which strike it either on the edge or in the centre. The other side of the Mridanga is left bare, but on every occasion when it is used, a mixture of boiled rice, water and ashes is put in the centre. This helps to give the dull sound *Panchama*. It must be carefully washed off every time after it is used. This head is played with the left hand. *

The drummer sits cross-legged upon the floor with the Mrudanga across his knees. In the case of the *Tabla* the two small drums stand upright in front of him, the drummer playing the tuned drumhead with his right hand and the other drumhead with his left. With the left hand he beats the main outline of the particular rhythm being used. With his right he performs a kind of rhythmic embroidery in the form of intermediate beats, or even cross-beats to the main rhythm. In this way an expert drummer can execute the most intricate and fascinating rhythms, and often commands a large fee for a single evening's performance.

There are many other kinds of drums used in India. Only the following are given special mention here. These are not tuned.

1. The *Dhol* (Dhavul). This is the drum which is generally used in temple worship and at weddings. It usually accompanies the Nagaswara and has been called the "wedding drum". Mr. Popley has described it as follows.

It is cylindrical in shape and about 20 inches long and 12 in diameter. It is made of wood bored out of the solid. The heads are made of skin and are stretched by hoops fastened to the shell and

* Popley, MUSIC OF INDIA, p. 120.

strained by interlaced thongs of leather bound round the shell. A band of leather passes round the shell in the middle and serves to tighten up the instrument to the desired pitch. A mixture of boiled rice and wood ash is often applied to the ends of the *dhol* to give more resonance. The drum is played either by hand or with sticks. Sometimes both are used. If by hand, it is struck by the palm. The sound is a hollow bang, with very little music in it, and there is no possibility of drumming finesse, as there is with the mridanga. *

2. The *Urumi.* This is a small drum commonly used in the village bands of South India. It is in general cylindrical in shape, but with a narrow neck in the middle, like an hour-glass. Each of its two drumheads is played upon with a single stick. These sticks are long and slender, and the one played by the left hand is curved. The drummer carries this drum tied to a rope hanging from his neck. While beating the upper drumhead with a stick in his right hand, he draws the curved stick with his left hand across the lower drumhead in a rubbing fashion. The result is a peculiar sound like "Boo-uh, boo-uh, boo-uh".

Other Percussion Instruments.

These may be described as various kinds of cymbals, castanets, and tambourines.

There is a small type of cymbals called the *Jalra* or *Kai-tala.* These are usually of brass. Some cymbals may be about five inches in diameter but are generally much smaller. Group singers often use them, and they are also used in the Kalakshepam. (See Chapters VII and VIII).

There is also a small tambourine called the *Kanjiri* in North India and the *Kanjira* in South India. It is six to eight inches in diameter. Experts can play very skillfully and attractively upon these.

For the *Bhajan* or the *Kalakshepam* the chief singer (bhagavathar), in order to keep the time, uses a pair of castanets made of wood, called in South India the *Sipplakattai.* They are made of one round piece of wood, such as rose-wood, by being turned on a lathe to give them their graceful shape, and then cut in halves. Each half has an inner flat surface and small jingle bells at each end. The singer holds a pair in one hand in such a way as to clap the castanets together to keep time, as in the case of cymbals. The main difference between the two types of cymbals is that in the case of the Jalra a cymbal is held in each hand, whereas the Sippla-kattai is manipulated by the thumb and fingers of one hand. A little practice will reduce the difficulty which one feels when one first tries to keep time with them.

* Popley, MUSIC OF INDIA, p. 122.

CHAPTER VII

THE KALAKSHEPAM, OR KIRTAN

The term Kalakshepam (or Katha-Kalakshepam, as it is also called) literally means, *passing the time.* In North and West India its name is *"Kirtan."* It is a kind of musical performance in which one person narrates a sacred story by telling it in both words and songs, each song reinforcing some phase of the story. The singer-preacher is accompanied by a small orchestra. The performance is usually in the evening, either inside a building or outdoors and lasts for several hours. The story chosen is from some sacred book, such as the Mahabharata or the Ramayana, or the Bible. From its origin the Kalakshepam seems to have been closely associated with religion. Its main purpose has been to furnish both entertainment and inspiration. Since religion is a matter of emotion as well as of intellect, one can easily understand how valuable this type of music can be in bringing about changes in human attitudes and conduct. In earlier chapters we have noted how powerful the effect of music is upon the hearts of Indians. An expert in the Kalakshepam can create by his music an atmosphere which will be exceedingly helpful for the presentation of a spiritual message. Western musicians also use their music with similar purpose and result.

There is very little literature on the subject of Kalakshepam, either in English or in the Indian languages. This is probably due to the fact that this art, as in the case of other types of Indian music, is largely the result of oral transmission rather than of books. In the year 1919 the Christian Literature Society of Madras published in the Tamil language a book on the Kalakshepam written by L. I. Stephens, an Indian minister, and Herbert A. Popley, an English missionary. Besides a brief introduction in English on the essentials of Carnatic music, the authors presented a number of songs based upon fifteen stories from the Bible, together with the notes of the songs in Indian notation. In 1932 Mr. M. S. Ramasamy, a noted Indian scholar and musician, published at Madras in English a pamphlet on the origin and growth of the Kalakshepam. Much of what is stated in this chapter is taken from that pamphlet. Both

45

these publications are listed in the bibliography at the end of this book. In 1955 the Christian Literature Society published a small book by the present author on the Kalakshepam.

If there are any other books in existence on this subject, I have not yet encountered them.

Like classical music, the origin of the Kalakshepam goes back to Vedic times. Centuries later it took on a more popular form. A whole village would gather outdoors in the evening in some central place to listen to a performance. The singer-preacher (*Bhagavathar*) would set forth glowingly the virtues of some Puranic hero or heroine, such as Prince Rama and his wife Sita. Epic stories have been immortalized in song, and sung all over India for centuries, and are still popular. By such performances the singer-preacher would hold his audience spellbound, while night after night, he developed the story and dramatized certain moral teachings. In those days the Kalakshepam did not suffer from competition with the counter-attractions of today. There was little popular literature, no newspapers, moving pictures, radio, or television. Travel to distant places was difficult or expensive.

Our knowledge of the Kalakshepam in ancient times is very limited. The Gupta kings of the first three centuries of the Christian era were said to have patronized "lectures" on the theme of *bhakti* (religious devotion). These lectures were conducted in temples and were interspersed with songs. At that time it is said that the Kalakshepam took a turn toward opera. Unfortunately little is known about the Gupta dynasty. As already noted, in the twelfth century a musician named Jeyadeva composed a lyrical poem entitled "Gita Govinda". With this the Kalakshepam assumed a new form.

When the Muslim invaders came to power in North India, the ancient Hindu music began to move southward, and the Kalakshepam went with it. Two centers became established for this ancient music. One was the Maratha country in the area of Bombay, and the other in Tanjore, now a city in Madras State, South India. The Kalakshepam, in another form, remained in North India, and had its ups and downs under the Muslim rulers.

It was in the Maratha country that the Kalakshepam underwent a special development. Many of the traditional tunes of South Indian Kalakshepam have had their origin in Western India. There are said to be fifteen or more of these tunes, each with one or more sub-tunes. (See the Appendix). It would be helpful in future if some musical expert would do research on this subject and unearth these tunes from the notebooks of various professional bhagavathars, and record these for posterity before the notebooks are destroyed and the tunes lost. Each of the tunes is based upon some raga, but is fairly simple and easily learned. We have already noted that in those days the power of the Maratha kings extended southward into what is now known as Mysore State and as far as Tanjore. Up to that time Tanjore was a center of Carnatic music and knew nothing of the Kalakshepam.

The man who should be remembered as the introducer of the Kalakshepam into South India was the famous singer, Krishna Bhagavathar of Tanjore (1847-1902). He visited in the Maratha country and learned its Kalakshepam tunes. Then he took the Carnatic music of South India, with its tediously long performances, and transformed it into a popular form by substituting the short, crisp tunes of the Maratha Kirtan. He is said to have been a master of the art of the Kalakshepam and to have had great dramatic power over his audiences.

Two other contemporaries of Krishna Bhagavathar are worthy of special mention here. One was **Lakshmanachariar** (1857-1920) of Tiruvaiyur and **Panchapakesa Sastri** (1868-1924) of Tirupayanam, both of South India. The former was outstanding because of the high spiritual quality of his performances, and the latter was noted as a profound Sanskrit scholar and for his helpful teachings.

In more recent times four Christian ministers (now no longer living) have deserved notice because of their attainments in the Kalakshepam. Since the author has not had the privilege of direct contact with the Kalakshepam in other parts of India, the following examples are taken from South India.

1. **Richard Hickling.** (1866-1934). He was an Englishman who worked under the London Missionary Society near Bangalore. He was a gifted preacher in Telegu and Kanarese, which are two of the Dravidian languages of southern India. In addition he possessed a knowledge of Sanskrit and of Hindustani, and could sing well. Finding that he could reach Indian audiences better by using Indian modes and rhythms in his preaching, he trained a band of Indian musicians to accompany his songs and chants. This type of preaching drew large audiences.

2. **Vedanayagam Sastriar.** (1884-1938). This gifted Indian was a descendant of the famous Vedanayagam Sastriar of Tanjore (already mentioned in Chapter II). He possessed unusual power over his audiences by his singing, was an effective speaker, and had a wide reputation. The author had the privilege of listening to him.

3. **T. Ayyadurai.** (1884-1948). He was the son of a learned Saivite of Tirunelveli District, S. India, who became a Roman Catholic convert. Ayyadurai was noted for his ability to compose the three kinds of Tamil literature: prose, poetry and dramatic verse. He was also commended for his fine singing voice and for the fact that he had a better knowledge of classical Indian music than many Indian Christians of his time. Before he died his fame had spread to Ceylon, Burma and Southeast Asia. The author had the pleasure of studying under his instruction for one year.

4. **Herbert A. Popley.** (1878-1960). He was an Englishman who worked in India under the London Missionary Society at Erode and Coimbatore, South India, excepting a period of seventeen years when his work was with the Young Men's Christian Association. He was distinguished for his intensive knowledge of Indian music. In addition to becoming co-author of a book on the Kalakshepam, he wrote a scholarly work on the music of India as a whole. (See bibliography). He often conducted Kalakshepams, singing and playing his own accompaniment on the violin. His memory is held in great affection among all Tamil musicians.

In contrast to the *Bhajan,* the Kalakshepam does not consist entirely of singing, nor is there any vocal participation on the part of the audience. It is really a case of one man preaching and singing, accompanied by musical instrumentalists. The ensemble includes the following:

1. The *Singer-preacher* (bhagavathar). To be a good Kalakshepam preacher calls for an unusual type of person. He must be well trained in Indian music. He must be able to stand, sing and speak for two or three hours at a time without losing the interest of the audience. It is he who sets the pace of a performance, stopping the music at any point in order to give the message in speech and in like manner resuming his song when he pleases. The singer-preacher stands throughout the performance, even if he is not at the moment himself singing, or preaching. All the remaining musicians, except one (the assistant singer), are seated around him on the floor of the platform.

2. The *Drone.* This may be the *Tambura,* but is often reinforced by a small organlike instrument called the *Sruti-patti* (pitch-box), which plays no tune but only the single drone chord or pitch. While the singer is preaching, all instruments, except the Drone, remain silent. The Tambura, or Sruti-patti, continues to sound softly during the speech, in order that the singer may have the pitch when he resumes singing. The drone chord also continues during the singing, and when the singer intones his message.

3. The *Violin.* A violin player who is skilled in the knowledge of ragas can add very effectively to the presentation of the message. While accompanying the melody with the singer-preacher, there will be times when the latter will pause for a minute or two while the violinist powerfully stresses the *raga bhava* (or the life) of the raga being sung or intoned. This helps greatly to create the musical background of the message. In this way the singer-preacher may be led to surpass his best efforts.

4. The *Drum.* This is a very important component of a Kalakshepam. As in the case of all concert instruments, the drum must be tuned. In South Indian performances the drum most used is the *mrudanga,* in North India it is the *tabla.* (See Chapter VI). The drum, like

the Tambura, must be carefully tuned well in advance of the performance. As in the case of the concert, there is at least one point at which the drummer will be able to display his skill in a solo performance, while the singer temporarily rests his voice.

5. The *Assistant Singer*. It is not compulsory for the singer-preacher to have an assistant singer, but it is preferred. There may be times when the former needs to rest his voice, or to pause temporarily during a song. The assistant then takes over for the time being. The two may frequently sing together, particularly in the chorus of a song.

A question may now arise as to the kind of songs to be used in a Kalakshepam. Mention has already been made of the traditional tunes. The bhagavathar should not be bound by hard-and-fast rules as to what kind of songs or tunes should be used. Any songs which, both as regards words and music are suited to his theme, may be useful. He may like to draw upon books of songs already published. These are, however, without any notation but with the appropriate modes and rhythms indicated. The late Vedanayagam Pillai, a village government officer, has composed a book of good spiritual songs in Tamil which may be used by adherents of any religion since they have no sectarian names. There are also hymnals of various kinds, and there are religious songs in the classical mode. Or, if the preacher-singer has the ability, he can compose his own songs. If he is not competent to do this, he can ask some skilled versifier to compose the words which he desires to use in a certain song at a particular phase of the story which he is to narrate. If he does not know a tune suitable for it, he may consult some musician to help him find one. It seems best that the traditional Kalakshepam tunes be used as the basis of the Kalakshepam, but that occasionally some popular tune, Hindi or other, or even a classical song, could be introduced if desired. Usually only a part of each song is, such as a verse and the chorus, since there will be frequent alternation between speaking and singing. This helps to maintain the attention of the audience.

The Kalakshepam follows a certain procedure, especially at the beginning and at the end. It opens with two songs of a general religious nature sung in succession. The first is a longer one called "Panjapati" ("panj" means "five" and "pati" means "God"). It has a series of five or more verses based upon five different ragas. The verses are in praise of God in whose honor the Kalakshepam is being conducted. The second song is very short and has for its theme the need of religious faith on the part of all people. After this the singer-preacher begins his introduction leading up to the narration of the story chosen. This introduction often opens with a few words intoned in the raga of the song just sung. It stresses the need for religious faith (bhakti). Near the end of this introduction the speaker pauses to sing another special song called "Tillana". This song is a kind of showpiece for the benefit of the drummer. It is

49

composed of words in praise of God, notes of the Indian *sol-fa* system, and of the sounds of the drum. While the singer-preacher sings this song, the drummer exhibits his skill, and receives a round of applause at the end. After this the preacher begins the story of the Kalakshepam, telling it phase by phase, each phase illustrated by a brief suitable song. If the performance lasts for two hours, he may sing parts of as many as 25 or 30 songs. The Kalakshepam concludes with an earnest appeal to the audience to live in accordance with the theme presented in the story. The performance then ends with the *Mangalam* song, in which Divine blessing is invoked upon the message thus presented.

Although the constituent elements of the Kalakshepam are important, a great deal also depends upon the ability and dedication of the singer-preacher. He will have a variety of hearers in his audience. There will probably be present an expert musician or two, as well as a number of persons who are well grounded in classical literature or in some intellectual subject. There will also be present many to whom music strongly appeals although they themselves may not be outstanding performers. Lastly there will be many folk who are neither musical nor intellectual but who enjoy humor and a good story. The singer-preacher will have to keep in mind all these different hearers. He may sometimes tell a humorous story by way of illustration. By his facial expressions and dramatic power he can arouse and maintain the interest of his audience.

Unless his over-all purpose is to entertain his audience, he will subordinate all his modes of expression to the purpose of driving home to his hearers some truth of high moral or spiritual order. The art of Kalakshepam is difficult, but this is true of every worthwhile undertaking. If by this art he succeeds in conveying his spiritual message, he will experience a sense of humility and of high privilege at being a channel of inspiration through the Kalakshepam.

CHAPTER VIII

TYPES OF FOLK MUSIC

Up to this point we have been concerned almost entirely with classical music. It is now necessary to take up the subject of more popular forms. It is significant that in the West at the present time there is some confusion of India's classical music with her popular music, since when one seeks to find recordings of India's classical music or her musical instruments, he is apt to find them all classified under the caption "Folk Music". This is a mistaken arrangement since classical music and folk music are not one and the same. As we shall see, there are many differences.

Folk music is probably the oldest and most universal form of music. Men sang even before musical instruments were invented. Folk songs constitute a primitive mode of expressing a human need. Human beings have a spontaneous, innate desire to express themselves in song and dance. Indians composed songs while they worked and when they danced or played. Even now in India when workmen strain to lift by hand a very heavy piece of timber, they often sing a chantey. Folk songs are associated with agricultural work, with games, and with such social events as weddings. Pilgrims will sing songs called "Chindus" while travelling to sacred places. Women sing while they pound unhusked rice with heavy pestles.

A folk song is subject to the following musical limitations:

a. It is bounded by the declamations of a ballad or by the stopping of a dance.

b. It is purely melodic, with usually no harmony parts and limited to notes within an octave.

c. It survives by being handed down vocally from generation to generation.

Books have been written to describe the folk music of many nations, particularly in the West, but that of yet many other nations and tribes remains to be studied. In this chapter three types of the folk music of India are set forth.

51

1. The *Kummi*. The Kummi is a song-and-dance performed without the use of musical instruments. The rhythm may be maintained by handclaps or some other means. When maintained by the striking together by each participant of a pair of brightly colored sticks, it is called *Kolattam*. The Kummi is a very old form of folk music and is very popular among women and girls. It may be described as follows:

Some twenty or more girls form a circle, standing one behind another. The performance is usually held at a time of day when it is cool. As a leader in the circle starts a song, the group repeats the line sung. As they sing they move forward in a circular direction, each girl clapping her hands in unison with the others. As each takes a step forward, she bends her body slightly downward and toward the inside of the circle and claps her hands once. The next step and handclap will be outward and to the right. In this way the girls move round and round in the circle, bending first inward and then outward and clapping their hands in unison to mark the time as they sing. It is a very common dance and very pretty to watch.

There are several other types of folk music performed by women and girls. In one of these flowers are arranged in brass vases, each arrangement being about two feet high. Each one of the girls places a vase on her head balancing it carefully as she sings, gracefully moving around the circle, swaying and clapping her hands in rhythm. One expects the flowers to topple in the middle of the dance, but they never do. In India the women frequently carry large pots of water from the well, or pieces of baggage on their heads as they walk, and this makes them very graceful in all folk dances. The subject matter of the songs deals with rural activities, such as the planting of rice, scenes in Nature, or any social events which may be occurring in the village. They may even compose on the spot words which pertain to some special passer-by. When the performance is a Kolattam, intsead of a Kummi, the procedure is much the same, except that the girls who stand in the circle face each other in pairs, each holding a pair of brightly colored sticks which they alternately beat together and then beat against the sticks of the opposite girl.

Boys also perform a kind of Kummi, but their performance is much more lively and vigorous. In the Madurai area of Madras State boys or young men will do what is called an *Oyil-Kummi*. They line up in ranks instead of in a circle. The leader will stand at one end of the front rank. On one ankle he wears an anklet with tiny jingling bells, which sound with every stamp of his foot. Each boy holds in his hand a small, square scarf, usually colored. As in the case of the regular Kummi, the leader sings a line and it is immediately taken up by the group. All the evolutions are performed in unison and very smartly. As each boy takes one step forward, then sidewise, then backward, he raises his right hand aloft and waves the scarf once with each beat. As the song and the step-taking proceed, the tempo quickens until the song and the various movements are executed with greater and greater speed. This keeps up until the group becomes breathless. Suddenly the leader blows his whistle and the song and dance stop at once. After an interval of rest another Kummi will be performed in the same way. It is a real physical "work-out" and, when well done, is as exciting to watch as an athletic contest.

2. The *Villadi-Pattu*. This is said to have originated among certain hill-tribes. It is undoubtedly a very ancient type of folk song. A long time ago some hunter, with bow and arrow, discovered that by beating upon the taut string of a strung bow he could perform a kind of rhythmic accompaniment to folk songs. In the course of time the Villadipattu evolved. The term means "a beating-upon-a-bow song". It is performed by five or more musicians. The singer soloist sits in the center of the group and immediately behind the long strung bow, which rests horizontally upon uprights with the bowstring uppermost. In his hands he holds two slender drumsticks. At each end of the bow and in the center of the bowstring hang a number of small jingling bells and various decorative ornaments. Sitting behind the singer and to his right or left sits a man who plays a small drum called the "Udukkai." A third musician plays upon a clay pot (*Gadam*) with his hands, by placing the open mouth of the pot against his bare abdomen and causing certain sucking sounds by alternately placing and pulling the mouth of the pot from his abdomen. A fourth musician will use a pair of cymbals. This type of song has been used both for instruction and for entertainment among illiterate rural people. The singer begins by singing a line of a song, and the refrain, or line, is immediately taken up by his companions in song and rhythm. As he sings the soloist will beat with his drumsticks upon the jingling bowstring. The main words of the song will be sung by the soloist only.

The Villadi-pattu has been known chiefly in the extreme south of India. It is said that it has been frequently found in the area of the villages in the Tirunelveli District during the summertime. Before the advent of political independence in India it seemed to be dying out. This was a great pity, for it had considerable educational value among illiterate people far from the conveniences and advantages of the great city, Since India attained independence, however, efforts have been made to develop this form of folk music in order to educate the villager in the subjects of public health, sanitation, social welfare, morals, and religion.

3. The *Bhajan*. This is a type of folk music used, not for entertainment, but for a means of corporate expression of the worship of some deity. It has been much used in several parts of India, especially in the western and southern parts. We have noted that the Kalakshepam consists of story and song by one man only, assisted by players on musical instruments. In the Bhajan, however, there is no speaking. All is done in song, and the soloist singer is assisted by a group of singers and accompanying instruments. The soloist sits on the floor of a platform, surrounded by some twenty or more singers and instrumentalists. He

sings a series of songs, one immediately following another, for an entire evening. First, he begins a song by intoning a line of religious devotion, accompanied only by the Drone instrument. Then he sings the first line of the song. This is immediately repeated by the entire group with the percussion instruments — mrudanga, or tabla, cymbals, and castanets joining in. Some of the group will keep time with cymbals or castanets and others will simply clap their hands in unison. Often members of the audience will participate in the group singing, both adults and even small children. The entire performance is made up of songs of religious praise and devotion. The songs may each be based upon some raga, but without the complexity of classical music. The soloist himself will hold in his hand a pair of castanets and join with the others in keeping time.

The Bhajan seems to have been highly developed in the Marathi-speaking country near Bombay. There the songs are associated with the worship of the Hindu god Vishnu. The music is highly emotional, the singers quickening the tempo as they sing each song, until at the end of the song it rises almost to a frenzy of religious devotion. As a line of the song is repeated several times, hands and cymbals are raised high over the heads of the group and beat a quickened tempo. The various names of the god — "Hari-Ram", "Hari-Krishna-Ram", "Govinda", etc. — are repeated over and over again. The program may last several hours. It usually takes place in the evening. The author was once a spectator at such a Bhajan on two successive evenings in a private home in Trivandrum, South India. Each evening it was in a different home. In one instance it was held in celebration of the birthday of the grandmother of the house. At each performance the house was filled to overflowing by an audience who listened with rapt attention and devotion. Every year Bhajans are conducted at Hindu religious festivals near the city of Poona in the months of July and October. Great crowds gather to listen. The songs are entirely religious and devotional. The very tunes used are such that they could not be mistaken for secular ones. As a result the effect of the songs upon the audience is not that of entertainment but of religious devotion.

CHAPTER IX

SELECTED SONGS IN STAFF NOTATION

The musician who plays these songs is requested to keep in mind the following points:

1. The songs have been recorded from the author's memory as he learned them orally from his teachers. They would not necessarily be sung exactly in the same way by professional Indian singers. The latter would render them with their own improvizations and embellishments. This is particularly true of classical music. Hence what is recorded here of each song is a kind of musical skeleton. Classical songs are much more difficult to record in staff notation than popular ones.

2. The *Drone Chord. This is the only harmony which should be used.* To indicate this, an appropriate chord, in the key of each piece, has been placed in the bass clef for each song. This chord should be maintained continuously throughout the song. Any attempt to play these songs by introducing Western harmonies will not represent them correctly.

3. The player is reminded that the indicated rhythm of each song must be maintained without pause from beginning to end, unless otherwise specified.

4. The first six songs are all in the classical mode; the remaining four are of the popular type. The words of the first four are in Telegu, a Dravidian language spoken in South India. The words and music were composed by the famous musician Tyagaraja. The fifth song is in the Sanskrit language and was composed by Muthusamy Dikshitar, another noted musician. All the first five songs are in praise of a Hindu god. The remaining five songs are recorded with words in Tamil, another Dravidian language. The first of these is a Christian hymn in the classical style. The next two may be classified as folk songs, and the last two are typical of the Kalakshepam.

5. At the head of each song the particular raga and tala on which the song is based are both indicated, the raga's name on the upper left and the tala's on the upper right. Classical songs have their divisions, entitled (in order) Pallavi, Anupallavi and Charanam. (See Appendix for terms.) Every classical song possesses all three of these divisions, but popular music does not necessarily contain all of them. The song begins and ends with the Pallavi. This may be considered as Chorus

55

One. It is followed by the Anupallavi which is Chorus Two. After singing the Anupallavi the singer repeats the Pallavi, then proceeds to sing the Charanam, and again returns to the Pallavi. It has not always been possible to indicate this procedure in the notation of the following songs.

6. The approximate sounds of the original words are given in romanized form under the notes of the songs. Each song is followed by either a translation of the words, or by the gist of the meaning. For pronunciation of the sounds of some of the Indian letters the reader should consult the Key to Pronunciation in the Glossary of the Appendix.

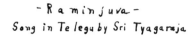

- Raminjuva -
Song in Telegu by Sri Tyagaraja

RA-MIN-JU-VA
by Tyagaraja
Translation by Vidwan D. Srinivasa Iyengar

(Pallavi)

O Thou Great One,

Born in the Raghu dynasty!*

Who save thee can give

Complete poise of mind?

(Anupallavi)

Thou art the Master of peace,

And of the Six Gunas.**

Who like thee can give complete tranquillity

To all peoples in all worlds?

(Charanam)

Thou are the god of Saint Tyagaraja.

Not even the angels can appreciate

The sweet word Rama

Nor pronounce his name.

---

*Family of Prince Rama.

**Divine attributes of omniscience, supremacy, pre-ordination, omnipresence, unlimited creative power, almightiness.

MARUKAYLARA

Telegu Song by Sri Tyagaraja

Raga: Jeyanta Sri (Pallavi) Tala: Adi

Ma-ru-kay-la-rä   Ah   Rä-gha-
vä   Ma-ru-kay-la-rä   Ah---
Ah--   Ma-ru-kay-la-rä   Ah
(Anupallavi) Ma-ru-kay-la cha-rä cha-ra-roo
Ma-ru-kay-la cha-rä cha-ra-roo Pa
rät--- Pa-ra-sür-ya süt-thä ka-ra-lö-
cha-na Ma-ru-kay-la-rä Ah------
(Charanam) An-ni-nï va-nut-su an-tha-rang-ga-
mu-na an-ni-nï--- va-nut-su an-tha-rang-ga
mu-na Tïn-na-gä vet-tha-gee Te-lu-su kon-di-
nai-yä nin-nay-gä ni-ma-thi-nay Nen-na-jä----
nin-nay-gä ni-ma-thi-nay Nen-na-jä no--
---ru-la Nan-nu-brö-va vai-ya Tyä-ga-rä-
ja-nu-tha Ma-ru-kay-la-rä Ah-------- fine

58

MA-RU-KAY-LA-RA
by Tyagaraja
Meaning of the song.

O Supreme One, why dost Thou hide thyself?

O Raghava!*

I have learned and realize that thou art

Everything in the world.

I have no thought in mind

Of anything else but thee!

O save me!

*Another name for Rama.

59

Yentha Nerchina

Telegu song by Sri Tyaqaraja

thä　Pa - ra je - va - na - moo

Pa - ra je - va - na - moo　An - dru tha

may　Pa -shim cher - rir Ai - yä　Tyä-ga - rä - ja-nu-

tha　Yen-tha ner - chi - nä　yen-tha sur - chi

nä　Yen-tha vä - ra lai - na　gän-tha dä - su-

lay　Yen- tha ner- chi - nä　*fine*

YEN-THA-NER-CHI-NA
by Tyagaraja
General Meaning

No matter how educated or learned one may be, unless he has bhakti*, he cannot approach God, nor fathom the godliness and activities of the Almighty. A knowledge of the Vedas will not produce a bhakta**. Only by godliness and a pure heart is this stage attained. Anyone audacious enough to imagine he can attain it by a first class education is a good-for-nothing! Not by learning but only through effort of will can this be done.

*See Glossary.
**See Glossary.

SAN-THAM U-LAY-KA
by Tyagaraja
General Meaning

*Even though one may possess
Wealth, wife and children,
And even though he prays,
If he does not have
A meek and tranquil mind,
He will not possess good health.*

– Vathapi –

Sanskrit Hymn by Muthusamy Dikshitar

(Charanam)

Pu-rā gum-ba-sam pa-va-mu-ni va-ra

Pra-bū-ji-tham dhru-kōr--na ma-dhya ha-tham

Mu-rā----rī pra-mu-gād dhyu pās-thi-tham

Mū-lā-thä-ra chēt-träs-thi-tham

Pa-rä-ri sat-thwä nru-vä häth-ma-ham

Pra-na-va sva-rū-pa va-kra thurn-dam-

Ni-ram-tha-ram nir-di-la san-thira harn-dam

Ni-ja-vä ma-ha-ra-vi thru-thē chū-tharn-dam

Kräm-pu-ja pä-sam pee-jä poo-ram Ka-lu-sha-pi dhū-ram poo-thä-hä-ram

D.C.al fine

Hu-rä-thi gu-ru-hu-ha dhō-shi-tha pim-bam Ham-sa Dwa-m poo-shi-tha-hay ram-bam

64

VA-THA-PI.
Sanskrit Hymn
Translation by Vidwan D. Srinivasa Iyengar

I worship Ganapati of Vathapi,*
Lord of the world and the Five Elements**
Adored by saints and yogis,
The Source of the universe
And Destroyer of suffering.
Adored he is by Vishnu
And by other gods.
He lives in the hearts of his worshippers,
Eternal and Center of all things.
He is one with the sound of "OM".***
On his brow is the moon,
His left hand bears a sugarcane,
Within his lotuslike palm
He carries a pomegranate.
Spotless and holy,
The idol of Lord Subrahmanya,
Hamsa Dwani Raga
Is his delight.
Such is Ganapati,
Whom I adore.

*Name of a village associated with Ganapati.
**Earth, water, fire, air, ethereal matter.
***A sacred symbol pronounced to create the mystic state of union with God.

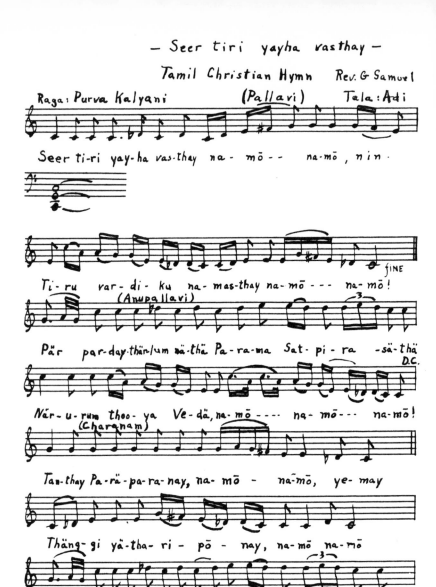
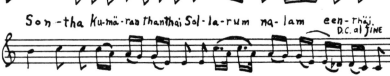

SEER   TI-RI   YAY-HA   VAS-THAY.

Tamil Christian Hymn
Composed by Rev. G. Samuel
Translated by E. E. White

(Pallavi)
Praise to thee, O Triune God!
Praise to thy holy foot!
(Anupallavi)
O Creator and Earth's Ruler!
O highest Food Divine!
O Revelation of holy love!
(Charanam)
Praise to thee,
O God the Father!
Praise to him
Who upholds and helps me!
Thou didst give
Thine only Son,
And didst grant to us
Blessings unspeakable,
And hast ended all our woes.

Tamil Song, "Ordi ordi" words by Siva Vakkiyar

Raga: Mohana   Tala: Misra Chapu

ōr-di ōr-di   ōr-di ōr-di   ut ka lan tha   Jō - - thee yay

Nār-di nār-di   nār-di nār-di   nārt kar-lum karlin   thu pōi

Vār-di vār-di   vār-di vār-di   marn - du pō na-mān tha - hurl

Kōr-di kōr-di   Kōr-di Kōr-di   yern ni-ran-tha Kōr - di - yay

ōr-di ōr-di   ōr-di ōr-di   ut ka lan tha Jō - - thee yay

Drone Chord

ORDI ORDI
Words by Siva Vakkiyar
Translated by E. E. White

Untold millions of people
Run and run,
Constantly seeking,
Grow desperate and die,
Looking for the light
That is within them.

Notes: "Ordi" means "runniňg"
          "Nardi" means "seeking"
          "Vardi" means "withering or fading"
          "Kordi" means (literally) "ten millions"

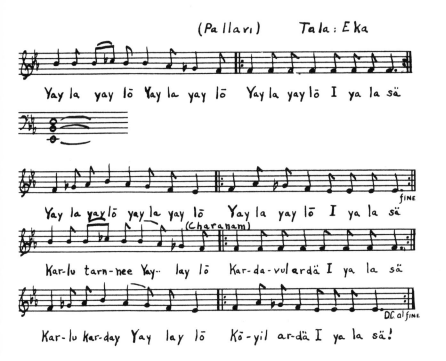

A Boating Song
Folk Song   Words by M. J. Daniel

(Pallavi)   Tala: Eka

Yay la yay lō Yay la yay lō Yay la yay lō I ya la sä

Yay la yay lō yay la yay lō Yay la yay lō I ya la sä

(Charanam)

Kar-lu tarn-nee Yay- lay lō Kar-da-vul ardä I ya la sä

Kar-lu Kar-day Yay lay lō Kō-yil ar-dä I ya la sä!

A BOATING SONG.
Folk Song, words by M. J. Daniel
General Meaning

The Pallavi is a common chantey composed of euphonious syllables sung in unison. In the Charanam only the syllables used in the Pallavi are sung in unison. The other words are sung by the leader. "Karlu tarnee" means "toddy," an alcoholic liquor from the fermented juice of the palmyra tree. "Kardavul" is the word for "God". "Karlu kardai" is the "toddy-shop", and "Koyil" means "church". This is a song which mocks those who drink to excess. It is often used in a Kalakchepam.
What the singer is saying in the Charanam is:
"Toddy is god, you fellow;
The toddy-shop is your temple, man."

69

- Bhakti Sayhuvom -
A Tamil Kalakshepam Song
Words by D. Arthur Bhagavathar

BHAKTI SAY-HU-VOM
Words by D. Arthur Bhagavathar
Translation by E. E. White

(Pallavi)
Let us, with words, melody and rhythm
Look up to God and practice bhakti.
(Anupallavi)
*In order that we may attain mukti**
'Tis important to control
*The three kinds of lusts.****

*"Mukti" is "heaven".
**Lust for land, lust for gold, lust for women.

70

TILLANA

By D. Srinivasa Iyengar

General Meaning

This cannot be translated literally because it is a mixture of the scale notes Sa-Ri-Ga, with sounds of the Mrudanga. This applies to both the Pallavi and the Anupallavi. In the Charanam the words, "I sing and praise the name of the Lord Jesus" are included with the same sounds. This song occurs early in a Kalakshepam before the story is begun and gives an opportunity for the drummer to display his skill.

APPENDIX

The Chromatic Scale, with Indian Nomenclature.

Note: The student should read upward from the bottom low C (Sa) to the upper C (Śa).

	(Carnatic Name)	(Hindustani Name)
Ċ (Ṡa) —	Shadja	— Shadja Ṡa
B (Ni) —	Käkali Nishäda	— Tīvra Ni
B♭ (ni) —	Kaisiki Nishäda	— Kōmal ni
A (Da) —	Chatusruti Dhaivata	— Tīvra Da
A♭ (da) —	Suddha Dhaivata	— Kōmal da
G (Pa) —	Panchama	— Panchama Pa
F♯(ma) —	Prati Madhyama	— Tīvra ma
F (Ma) —	Suddha Madhyama	— Kōmal Ma
E (Ga) —	Antara Gändhära	— Tīvra Ga
E♭ (ga) —	Sädharana Gändhära	— Kōmal ga
D (Ri) —	Chatusruti Rishaba	— Tīvra Ri
D♭ (ri) —	Suddha Rishaba	— Kōmal ri
C (Sa) —	Shadja	— Shadja Sa

The Carnatic ("Just") Scale and the Western ("Tempered") Compared

(Reading from bottom to top, and showing the 22 microtones)

(Number of Microtone)	(Scale of C)	(Indian Symbol)	(Western Cyclic Cents)	(Indian Cyclic Cents)
22 —	C —	Ṡa —	1200 —	1200
21 —	C♭ —	ni⁴ —		— 1110
20 —	B —	Ni³ —	1100 —	1088
19 —	B♭ —	ni² —	1000 —	1018
18 —	A♯ —	ni¹ —		— 996
17 —	A —	Da⁴ —	900 —	906
16 —	A♭ —	da³ —	800 —	889
15 —	A♭♭ —	da² —		— 814
14 —	G♯ —	da¹ —		— 792
13 —	G —	Pa —	700 —	702
12 —	G♭ —	ma⁴ —		— 610
11 —	G♭♭ —	ma³ —		— 590

72

10	F#	ma²	600	520
9	F	Ma¹	500	498
8	Fb	ga⁴		408
7	E	Ga³	400	386
6	Eb	ga²	300	316
5	D#	ga¹		244
4	D	Ri⁴	200	204
3	Db	ri³	100	182
2	Dbb	ri²		112
1	C#	ri¹		90
0	C	Sa	0	0

SELECTED CARNATIC RAGAS.

The following is a selected list of Carnatic ragas, each with its characteristic ascending (Arohana) and descending (Avarohana) notes. In many cases the traditional time of day when it is to be used, and the particular mood or passion, are indicated. Wherever possible, the corresponding name of the same raga in the Northern (Hindustani) School is given in parentheses. The ragas are divided into two groups: the 72 Primary, or parent, ragas, and the Secondary, or derivative, ragas. With each Secondary raga the number of its Primary raga is also indicated.

The total number of Secondary ragas is said to be limitless. Actually some 250 ragas are in common use in Carnatic music. The following list is not complete, but contains only some of the more common ragas.

In practising the singing of these ragas the student is urged to use the Sa- Ri- Ga notation as far as possible. Under an expert teacher he will sing the ascending and descending characteristic notes in the form of raga exercises (Varnas) with Tala and varying tempo. It should also be noted that, except for the notes of the drone chord, Sa- Pa- Sa, any of the intervening notes may be slightly sharper or flatter in pitch, according to the particular raga.

PRIMARY RAGAS

1. Hanuma-tōdi. No. 8. (Bhairavi).   Morning: sadness.
   This raga has a sound similar to that of the western chromatic scale.

2. Mäyä-imälava-goula. No. 15. (Bhairav).   Dawn: reverence.

3. Sūriya-känta. No. 17.

4. Nada Bhairavi. No. 20. (Sindhu-Bhairavi).   Night: sadness.
   Characteristic notes: Mä Gä Mä. These are stressed.

5. Kharahara-priya. No. 22.   At all times: Passion anger.
   This is the Dorian Mode. It approximates the Säma Gäna scale, a
   delight to Siva.

6. Hari-kämbōdhi. No. 28. (Jhinjhoti).   At all times: imploring.
   The Hypo-Lygian Plagal Mode.
   This raga differs from No. 29 mainly in having a flattened Seventh.

7. Dīra Sankaräbharana. No. 29. (Bilaval).   Morning: calm.

8. Gamana-priya. No. 53. (Märva).   3 to 6 p.m.: passion.

9. Mecha Kalyäni. No. 65.   At all times, but especially evening:
   merriment.
   Often used at the beginning of a concert.
   This is the Lydian authentic mode with the addition of F-Sharp.

SECONDARY (OR JANYA) RAGAS

(In alphabetic order) The primary raga from which each is derived is indicated by the letter P and a number.

1a. Ānanda Bhairavi. P.20.   Morning: for religious songs. This raga has a second set of characteristic notes, given below. Either may be used.

1b. Ānanda Bhairavi. P.20. E-Natural, A-Flat, and B-Natural also occur.

2. Arabhi. P.29.   All times: joy and devotion.

3. Atäna. P.28.   Noon: anger. E-Flat and B-Flat may occur.

4. Bhairavi. P.20.   6 to 10 p.m.

5. Bilahari. P.29.   6 to 10 a.m.: joy. B-Flat may occur. Drives away melancholy and disease. Often used for weddings.

6. Būpäla. P.15.   2 to 6 a.m.: worship of God.

7. Danyäsi. P.8. (Bhairavi).   Morning: pleading.

77

8. Dēvagändhäri. P.29.   2 to 6 a.m.: heroism.

9. Hindōlam. P.8. (Malkos).   2 to 6 a.m.: joy, love songs.

10. Jēyantha Srī. P.20.   At all times: devotion, (bhakti)

11. Jōn-puri Säikki. P.20.   At any time.

12. Kalyäni. P.65.   All times. Best in the evening: merriment.
Sometimes G is omitted.

13. Kämbōdhi. P.28. (Khamaj).   10 a.m. to 2 p..m.: praise.
Useful raga for intoning poetry.

14. Käphi. P.22.   10 a.m. to 2 p.m.: joy, bhakti.

15. Kēdära-goula. P.28.   Evening: kindness, tenderness.

16. Kuntha-varäli. P.28.   At all times: joy, wonder.

79

17. Madhyamävathy. P. 22. (Saranga). At all times: for songs of meditation.

18. Mēgh Ranjani. P.15. The "rain" raga.

19. Mukhäri. P.22. At all times: grief, sadness.

20. Näda-näma-kriya. P.15. (Kalangadi) Popular in songs of devotion.

21. Nilämbari. P.29. 10 a.m. to 2 p.m.: devotional songs, lullabies. A-Flat also occurs.

22. Panthu-varäli. P.45. Evening: adoration.

23. Punnäga-varäli. P.8. At all times: sorrow. Raga used by the snake charmer. On occasion D-Natural and E-Flat with a still flatter tone is sung.

24. Pūrva Kalyäni. P.53. Evening: loneliness, detachment from the world.

25. Sämä. P.28. At all times: bhakti.

26. Sahänä. P.28.   Tenderness.
    Sometimes E-Flat occurs.

27. Sävēri. P.15. (Jogiya).   2 to 6 a.m.: tenderness.

28. Sourāshtra. P.17.   At any time: blessing.
    B-Flat may occur. Used to invoke the divine blessing at the close
    of a Kalakshepam.

29. Srī. P.22.   Evening is the best time: sadness, asking forgiveness.

30. Subōshini. P.28.   At all times.

31. Utheyara Visanthirika. P.22.   At any time.

32. Vasantha. P.16. (Vasanth).   Evening: loneliness.

33. Vijēya Srī. P.45.   Pathos.

SELECTED HINDUSTANI RAGAS

(Taken by permission from H. A. Popley's MUSIC OF INDIA, pages 53-62, with several other ragas added, and amended by Mr. Amiya Das Gupta.)
Note: The appropriate time of day or night and the characteristic mood are indicated wherever possible. In cases where the name of the corresponding Carnatic raga is known, this is included in parentheses. Notes to be shaken are not indicated.

A modern expert of the Hindustani school claims that musicians of that school are stricter in the observance of the time of day at which a particular raga should be performed, than are the musicians of the more orthodox Carnatic school.

Hindustani ragas are subdivided into Primary and Secondary ragas, but no attempt has been made in this book to classify them.

1. Abhōgi. (Abhōgi).   9 p.m. to midnight: bhakti, entreaty.

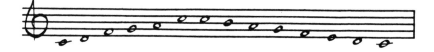

2. Adana. (Atana).   Third part of the night: pride.

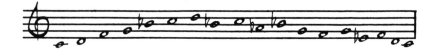

3. Ärabhi. (Ärabhi).   Night

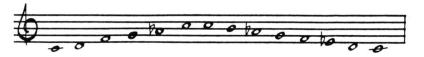

4. Asävari. (Nadabhairavi).   Morning: tenderness, renunciation.

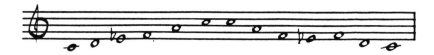

5. Basant. (Vasantha). At night, except during the season of Vasant Ritu: joyful.

6. Bhairava. (Mäyä-mälava-goula). Morning: tenderness, invocation.

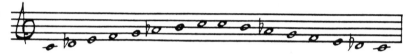

7. Bhairavi. (Hanuma-tōdi).　　　Morning: sadness, passion.

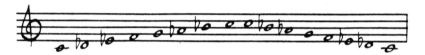

8. Bhimpalasi.　　　Afternoon: peace, tenderness.

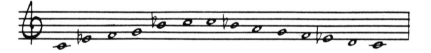

9. Bhoop.　　　First part of night. (Very popular).

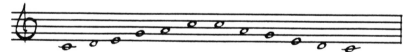

10. Bihag. (Bihäg).　　　Midnight: melancholy, desire for enjoyment.

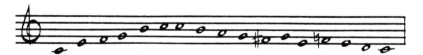

85

11. Durga. (Suddha Sävēri). Morning.

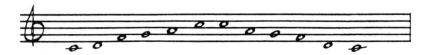

12. Dhanasri. Afternoon: calm.

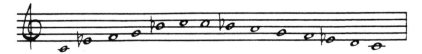

13. Gauri. Afternoon: laughter.

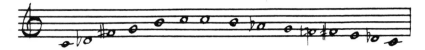

14. Hindol. 9 a.m. to noon in springtime: passion.

15. Jhinjhoti. (Senchurutti). Night: love.

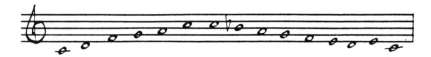

16. Khamäj. (Hari-kämbōthi, or Khamäj). Any time: love.

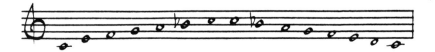

17. Kamoda.　　First quarter of night: pleasure, entertainment.

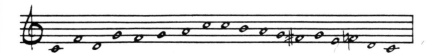

18. Kafi. (Kharahara-priya).　　　　　Morning: passion.

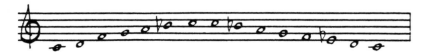

19. Kēdära. (Kēdära).　　Early part of night: pleasure, tenderness.

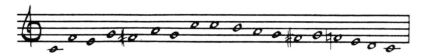

20. Gändhäri. (Gändhärava).　　　　　Evening.

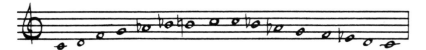

21. Lalita. (Süriyakänta).　　　　Night: tenderness.

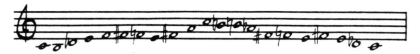

22. Malkos.　　Midnight, but also mid-day: peace, sublimity.
　　(Very popular).

23. Marva. (Gamanapriya). Before sunrise: roughness, uneasiness.

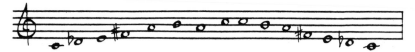

24. Multani. Second part of the afternoon: tenderness.

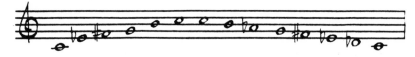

25. Purvi. (Kamavardhani). Last quarter of day: prayer.

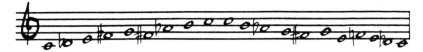

26. Saranga. (Madhyamävathi). Noon: gentleness, selflessness.

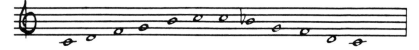

27. Srī. Last quarter of day: tenderness, melancholy.

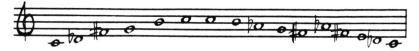

28. Tilanga. Night: quiet.

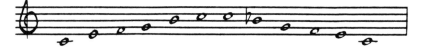

29. Yaman. (Mecha-Kalyäni). Second half of night: merriment.

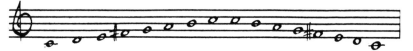

TABLE OF TALAS (RHYTHMS) IN CARNATIC MUSIC

(Taken from Page 75 of Popley's Music of India, by permission).

(Jati—Sub-division)

Name of Tala

		Chatusra (1) (Tisra-2) (Misra-3) (Khanda-4) (Sankirna-5)			
1. Eka Tala	4	3	7	5	9
2. Rupaka Tala	2.4	2.3	2.7	2.5	2.9
3. Jhampa Tala	4.1.2	3.1.2	7.1.2	5.1.2	9.1.2
4. Triputa Tala	4.2.2	3.2.2	7.2.2	5.2.2	9.2.2
5. Mathya Tala	4.2.4	3.2.3	7.2.7	5.2.5	9.2.9
6. Dhruva Tala	5.2.4.4	3.2.3.3	7.2.7.7	5.2.5.5	9.2.9.9
7. Ata Tala	4.4.2.2	3.3.2.2	7.7.2.2	5.5.2.2	9.9.2.2

THE TRADITIONAL KALAKSHEPAM TUNES, OR MELODIES

(As imported into South India from West India)

1. Patham. 2. Sakki. 3. Dindi. 4. Aphangam. 5. Panjasamaram.
6. Santhas. 7. Kanatchari. 8. Anja-nagitham. 9. Katka. 10. Sainthavi.
11. Tirupat. 12. Tillana. 13. Arya. 14. Ovi. 15. Pujanga Pirapakam.

BIBLIOGRAPHY

(Note: The list given below is not exhaustive but includes some of the more generally known books. Works in English are mainly cited. There are many other books, some of which are written in one or other of the Indian languages.)

Books of a Less Technical Nature.

Dolly Rizvi. *Great Musicians of India.* Crescendo Pub. Co., Boston. 1968.

S. Krishnaswamy. *Musical Instruments of India.* Crescendo Pub. Co., Boston. 1967.

Shahinda. *Indian Music.* Marsh and Company, Coupil Gallery, 5 Regent Street, London S.W. England. 1914, 96 pp. Written from the viewpoint of North Indian music.

Ethel Rosenthal. *Story of Indian Music and Its Instruments.* W. M. Reeves, 83 Charing Cross Road, London. 1928.

D. Radhajar. *The Rebirth of Hindu Music.* Theosophical Publishing House, Adyar, Madras, 1928.

Margaret Cousins. *The Music of the Orient and the Occident.* N. S. Paul and Company, 12 Frances Joseph Street, Madras, S. India, 1935.

S. R. Kuppuswami. *Short Survey into the Music of North and South India.* Printed at Workman Place, Avanashi Road, Coimbatore, S. India. 90 pages. First edition 1948.

Ravi Shankar. *My Music, My Life.* Simon and Schuster, New York, 1968.

R. K. Prabhu. *Indian National Songs.* Crescendo Pub. Co., Boston. 1966.

O. Gosvami. *The Story of Indian Music.* Asia Publishing House, Madras, S. India, 1961.

Books of a More Technical Nature.

A. H. Fox-Strangways. *Music of Hindustan.* Clarendon Press, Oxford, England, 1914. Written from the viewpoint of North Indian music. Very comprehensive and scholarly. (Out of print).

Captain C. R. Day. *Music of Southern India.* A large book now out of print. A few copies available at a high price. Can be found in some Indian libraries.

Chinnasamy Mudaliar. *Oriental Music in European Notation.* Printed at Ave Maria Press, Pudupet, Madras by Ayyasamy Iyer, first edition in 1928. Folio size in 302 bound pages. Has notes in English, Telegu and Tamil. (Out of print but obtainable in a library in Madras.)

Herbert A. Popley. *Music of India.* Crescendo Pub. Co., Boston, Mass. First edition 1921, revised 1951, third edition 1966. An excellent all-round study.

Alain Danielou. *Introduction to the study of Musical Scales.* Vol. I, pages 99-157 on *Modal Music of the Hindus.* Indian Society, 5 Victoria Street, London S.W.1 Vol. II. *Northern Indian Music: The Main Ragas.* Published under the auspices of UNESCO, Halcyon Press, London, 1954. 248 pages.

P. Sambamoorthy. *South Indian Music,* a series of small but scholarly works in paperback published from the year 1948 by the South India Publishing House, 4 Bunder Road, Georgetown, Madras, S. India.

Same Author. *Great Composers,* in two small paperback volumes published by the Indian Music Publishing House, Georgetown, Madras in 1950 and 1954, respectively.

Same Author. *A Dictionary of South Indian Music and Musicians,* a series of volumes about 165 pages each published by the Indian Music Publishing House, Madras-1, India, from 1952 onwards.

C. Subrahmanya Ayyar. *Grammar of South Indian (Karnatic) Music.* Published by the author at 46 Edward Elliot Street, Mylapore, Madras. 1st edition 1939, 2nd edition 1951. Deals with the physics and mathematics of South Indian music. Very technical.

G. H. Ranade. *Hindustani Music: Outline of Its Physics and Aesthetics.* Published at Bhave's New Wada, Old Town, Sangli, Bombay State, India.

M. S. Ramasamy. *Swara Mela Kalanidhi.* A translation from the Sanskrit by the author. Published at Annamalai University, Chidambaram, S. India in 1932. 66 large pages. Out of print.

C. Kunban Raja. *Sangita Ratnakara of Sarngadeva, Chapter I.* Translated from the Sanskrit by Subbarayada. Vedanta Press, Madras. 1945.

O. C. Gangoli. *Ragas and Raginis, Vol. I.* Published at S. Anbu Mukerji Road, Elgin P.O., Calcutta, 1947.

Mrs. S. Vidya. *Krithis of Syama Sastri, Subbaraya Sastri and Annaswami Sastri,* with Sa-Ri-Ga in Sanskrit and Tamil notation with Gamaka signs. Published by C. S. Ayyar at 46 Edward Elliot Road, Mylapore, Madras.

Books on the Kalakshepam.

In English.

M. S. Ramasamy. *The Kalakshepam, its Origin, Growth, Etc.* This is a small pamphlet published in 1932 by Selden and Company, Madras S.E. The author was a learned musician. It is not known whether the pamphlet is now available.

In Tamil.

Stephen and Popley. *Handbook of Musical Evangelism.* The introduction contains a small useful summary in English of the fundamentals of Indian music. This is followed by sets of model songs in Tamil based on fifteen different Bible stories. Tunes are in Indian notation. Published by the Christian Literature Society, Park Town, Madras, in 1919.

Emmons E. White. *The Kalakshepam as a Method of Evangelism.* Small book of 90 pages containing instruction on the technique of the Kalakshepam, together with a model for performance with twenty-two songs in Indian notation. A number of the traditional Kalakshepam tunes are used. Published by the Christian Literature Society, Park Town, Madras, in 1955.

GLOSSARY OF TERMS USED,
WITH KEY TO PRONUNCIATION.

Note about the Vowels: (As a rule the diacritical marks used are from Webster's Dictionary.)

"a" has the sound of "a" in "sofa".

(There is no "a" in Tamil which has the sound of "a" in "flat".)

"ä" is pronounced like the "a" in "father".

"e" has the sound of "e" in "pet".

"ē" has the sound of "a" in "may".

"i" has the sound of "i" in "pin".

"ī" has the sound of double "ee" in "feet".

"ŏ" has the sound of "o" in "obey".

"ō" has the sound of "o" in "note".

"u" has the sound of "u" in "put".

"ū" has the sound of "oo" in "pool".

The consonant "r" is always slightly trilled, except when it comes before the consonants "l", "n" and "d". Then it has its usual sound in English.

* * * * * * * *

Ädi. A measure containing eight time-units.

Akshara. A single time-unit, or beat.

Äläp. The introductory intoning of the raga of a song without rhythm. (Northern)

Äläpana. The Southern name for Alap.

Anga. A time-member within a measure or bar.

Antara Gändhära. Third note in the scale. (Southern)

Anudruta. A time-member with only one time-unit, or beat, indicated by a single handclap.

Anupallavi. The second of the three parts of a Carnatic song.

Ärōhana. Characteristic ascending notes of a raga.

Avarōhana. Descending characteristic notes of a raga.

Äti-kōmal. A double flat of a note in the scale. (Northern)

Ävarta. A measure or time-bar.

Bambai. A kind of small drum.

Bhajan. Concert of religious songs by a soloist with accompanying singers and instruments.

Bhägavathar. A soloist singer, artist.

Bhärata. Name of ancient India.

Bin. A North Indian instrument like the Vina.

Brahmä. The Creator, the first of the triad of Hindu gods.

Brähman. Member of the highest Hindu caste.

Cärnatic. Name of area from the Kistna River southward to Cape Comorin.

Chäpu. Rhythm maintained by handclaps or cymbal, and not by finger-count.

Charanam. Third of the three parts of a Carnatic song.

93

Chatusra. Number four.
Chatrusruti Dhaivata. Sixth note (Da) of the scale. (Southern)
Dhavul. The wedding drum. (Southern)
Dhōl. Northern name for Dhavul.
Dēva. God.
Drupad. A Northern type of song.
Druta. A time-member consisting of a handclap, followed by a hand-wave. (Southern) Also: the fast speed in music.
Drone. The characteristic sustained pitch or chord in Indian music.
Ganapati. The elephant-headed god (elder son of Siva).
Gāndhāra. Third note of scale.
Ganēsh. Another name for Ganapati.
Gīta. A simple song.
Hanumän. God-king of the monkeys.
Hindustäni. A colloquial form of Hindi. Also the name of the Northern School of Indian music.
Jalatarangam. ("Jalam" means "water"). A set of china bowls, which, when filled with water at different levels, can be used as instruments to play tunes.
Jälrä. A pair of small brass cymbals.
Jampai. A type of rhythm. (Southern)
Jäti. One of the five divisions of Täla.
Kaisiki. The flattened Seventh note (nī) of the scale.
Käkali. The Natural Seventh (Nī) of the scale.
Kälakshēpam. The song-sermon. (Southern)
Kälam. Any one of the three speeds of Indian music.
Khayal. A type of Northern song.
Kīrtan. The Northern name for Kälakshēpam.
Kīrtana. Name of a Southern song.
Kōl-ättam. A kind of folk-dance, performed by women.
Kōmal. A flattened note in the Northern scale.
Krishna. One of the ten incarnations of the god Vishnu.
Kriti. A type of classical song. (Southern)
Kummi. A folk-dance.
Laghu. A time-member consisting of a handclap followed by two or more fingerbeats.
Layam. A name for rhythm. (Southern)
Madhyama. The Fourth note (Mä) of the scale. Also the middle speed in music.
Mahä. Great.
Mandra. Lower tone register.
Manō-dharma Sangīta. Improvised music.
Mēla. (Pronounced "Mērla"). Name applied to a Primary Räga.
Misra. The number seven.
Mrudanga. The concert drum of South India.
Murali. Flute.

94

Nāgaswara. ·A South Indian wind instrument.
Nātaka. Drama.
Nātya. Artistic, interpretive dancing.
Ņishāda. Seventh note (Nī) in the scale.
Ōttu. An oboe-like reed instrument which plays a single sustained key-note.
Pallavi. The first of the three parts of a Carnatic song. (Similar to the chorus in Western music.)
Panchama. The Fifth note (Pä) of the scale.
Partial. One of the basic components of an ordinary note. A harmonic.
Prati Madhyama. The sharpened Fourth (mä) of the scale. (Southern)
Räg. A kind of musical scale on which a melody is based. (Northern)
Rāga. Southern name for a Räg.
Rāma. A legendary prince, worshipped as one of the ten incarnations of Vishnu.
Rāga Bhāva. The heart or life of a räga.
Rishi. A sage, or hermit.
Rūpaka. A measure, or time-bar, containing six time-units.
Sädhärana Gändhära. The flattened Third note (gä) of the scale. (Southern)
Sahitya. The words of a song. (Southern)
Sanchära. A string of non-rhythmic musical phrases of a räga.
Sangati. A series of rhythmic notes in a räga.
Sankīrna. The number seven.
Sannyäsi. A wandering religious ascetic.
Särangi. The Indian violin. (Northern)
Saivism. The worship of Siva as God.
Sarōd. A Särangi played with the plectra instead of the bow.
Shadja. The tonic or first note (Sä) of a scale.
Shenai. A small wind instrument. (Northern)
Sitär. A Northern stringed instrument similar to the Vīna.
Siva. The Destroyer. The third member of the triad of Hindu gods. In North India the name is spelled "Shiva".
Sruti. (1) A particular tonal pitch.
       (2) The basal pitch (Sä) of a performance.
Sruti-patti. Literally, pitch-box. A small wind instrument which plays only the drone-chord. A harmonium.
Stäyi. An octave, or register.
Suddha Dhaivata. The flattened Sixth note (dä) of the scale. (Southern)
Suddha Madhyama. Natural Fourth note (Mä) of the scale. (Southern)
Suddha Rishaba. Flattened Second note (rī) of the scale. (Southern)
Swara. A note of the scale.
Tabla. The Northern counterpart to the Mrudanga.
Täla. A type of rhythm.
Tambura. The stringed instrument for the drone-chord.
Tära. The higher octave, or register.

Tillänä. A kind of song used to demonstrate the Mrudanga in a Kalakshepam. Also used in dance music.

Tīvra. A sharpened note in the scale. (Northern)

Trisra. The number three.

Udukkai. A kind of small drum. (Southern)

Urumi. A small drum with a peculiar sound. (Southern)

Vaishnavism. The worship of Vishnu as God.

Varna. A vocal exercise in the singing of a räga.

Vidwän. A learned man, artist.

Vilamba. The slow speed in music.

Vīna. An ancient stringed instrument. (Southern)

Vishnu. The Preserver. Second in the triad of Hindu gods.